On Freedom's Altar

ON
FREEDOM'S
ALTAR

The Martyr Complex in the
Abolition Movement ⤳ By
Hazel Catherine Wolf

Madison—1952
UNIVERSITY OF WISCONSIN PRESS

To

WILLIAM BEST HESSELTINE

Preface

OF ALL the questions conducive to intersectional dispute in the United States in the years between 1830 and 1860, that of chattel slavery was actually least involved with differences in the fundamental needs and interests of the North and South. Since the early days of the republic the political representatives of Northern and Southern states had differed over the levying of tariff, over the establishment of a national bank, over the proper disposition of western lands, and over the expenditure of federal funds for internal improvements and the subsidization of the merchant marine. Time after time Northerners saw each suggested solution as it would affect a populous community in process of developing an industrialized economy, while Southerners concerned themselves with possible results for an agricultural society devoted to the production of a few staples. In the halls of congress and upon public platforms tempers flared as politicians accused each other of sectional selfishness on all the great questions. Nevertheless, during the first half of the nineteenth century Americans steadily approached workable solutions to all their intersectional differences—solutions which might have proved both equitable and lasting had they not been pursued in an atmosphere fraught with tension over slavery. For in the thirty years preceding the Civil War the abolitionists made that of the Negro's servitude the most disquieting of all issues. Propagandists in the best tradition of the term, they were bold, fearless, convinced of their own infallibility on every phase of the bondage question. They believed slave-keeping a moral issue, decried its sinfulness, dedicated themselves as their brothers' keepers and steadfastly worked to save both slave and master from the evil. For thirty years they drummed for their cause, tirelessly insisted upon prior consideration for abolition measures and constantly minimized the importance of solutions to other conflicts so long as the Negro remained in slavery.

Moreover, the abolitionists' recognition of the slave as a person gave meaning to their whole crusade. Their emphasis upon the dignity of man and the indignity of his enslavement coincided with the American ideal of freedom and equality. The most fiery speech full of the abstractions involved in any or all of the other questions in disagreement between the sections had little of the appeal which Theodore Dwight Weld made with his call to right wrongs done by Southerners who, as he claimed in *American Slavery As It Is,* punished their overworked, ill-fed, ill-clothed, and ill-housed slaves by means as fantastic as they were cruel. Pleas for the abstract rights of either section paled beside Weld's account of Southern masters who strung up fractious slaves by the thumbs and then beat them till they bled, who drew the slave's bound wrists so far over his knees that a rod could be passed above the arms and under the knees to place the victim in a position more advantageous for the master's lashing of the naked body. Men who would not hear an attack upon the political wrongs suffered by Northerners raged at Weld's account of planters whose atrocities included tying large cats to a slave's body, then baiting the frightened animals until they clawed and scratched the unfortunate victim whose wounds the master then bathed in brine. They became no less indignant at Weld's stories of Southerners who beat female slaves for resisting their lust, who ordered pregnant women to heavy field work, and returned them to those duties immediately after childbirth. Faced with so many flagrant violations of Christian and democratic precepts, many lost sight of economic and politi-

cal issues as the abolitionists called upon them to cast out slavery
for its disregard not only of human rights but even of human
life.

So while the abolition of slavery constituted but one among
many nineteenth-century reform movements, the abolitionists'
identification of the institution with sin and their emphasis
upon its inhumanity brought to their campaign an earnestness
and a zeal not so characteristic of those concerned with proper
Sabbath observance, recognition of women's rights, preparedness for the millennium, the salvation of temptation-plagued
sailors, the extension of temperance, or the rehabilitation of
prostitutes. Moreover, their concept of slavery as a national sin
led them to adapt to their own crusade the techniques of the
religious evangelists and they capitalized upon American re-
sponsiveness to appeals for recognition of evil and participation
in its rout. Abolition lecturers fired their audiences to reject
slavery and called forward all those converted and ready to join
the holy battle against it. In their wake men banded together
for zealous efforts for the Negro's freedom.

Yet despite the courage and zeal of the abolitionists, violent
opposition harassed them during their long crusade, for to many
Americans their appeal was as dangerous as it was disquieting.
Some saw in the movement the threat of northward migrating
Negroes who would claim the white man's job, become his
neighbor and social equal, perhaps even an aspirant for his
daughter's hand in marriage. Businessmen feared abolitionist
criticism would drive their Southern customers to purchase elsewhere. Established clergymen resented the itinerant abolition
preachers who, unannounced and uninvited, often divided their
congregations into proslavery and antislavery forces. Candidates
for political office dreaded the abolitionist questioners with
their demands for commitment on the slavery question. From
these opposition groups came men aplenty to resist the crusaders
and to provide them opportunities to suffer for cause. Hence
during the thirty years of the antislavery crusade Americans
heaped merciless punishment upon the abolitionists. Some

heckled them as they lectured to prospective followers, some attacked them verbally from pulpit and press while others beat, stoned, tarred and feathered them, drove them from public and private buildings, and denied them the protection of the laws—all because so many Northerners believed abolitionists were troublemakers rather than humanitarians. Convinced that if they met opposition with courage they demonstrated their sincerity, that if they bore their sufferings in patience they proved they enjoyed God's favor, the abolitionists continued in the face of all adversity and gave their crusade fire and momentum while other reforms and reformers faltered.

Indeed, reaction to the abolition crusade carried Americans through a wide range of human emotion. While the persecution of antislavery agitators brought tears to some sympathizers, it moved others to violent anger. For many years the majority of citizens saw in the antiabolition mobs the defenders of law and order battling contentious busybodies whose program encouraged hatred, murder, amalgamation, and rape instead of the humanitarianism which the crusaders said they espoused. After some abolitionists actually died for their cause, however, Northerners turned the hatred which some bore for slavery and which others had for abolitionists upon the perpetrators of the unhappy situation—the slaveholders in the South. During the latter half of the agitation period, therefore, emphasis upon the slaveholders' responsibility for the persecution of the crusaders for freedom brought both sections to emotional preparedness for fratricidal war.

Moreover, contributing factors in this preparation were the hundreds of orators who arose to champion each of the men who gave his life for his abolition beliefs. For Elijah P. Lovejoy, for Charles T. Torrey, for Old John Brown, ministers, laymen, and politicians quoted the Bible and other masterpieces of the world's literature and compared the contemporary situation with similar events in the history of other civilizations. Their long, wordy dissertations abounded in figures of speech, exclamatory remarks, and rhetorical questions. All over the North men heard these eulogies of abolition martyrs sacrificed to the inhumanity of the slaveholders and the conviction grew that there could be no peace in America until Southerners lived according to the Christian and democratic principles espoused by Northerners.

American abolitionists had been thorough in their campaign to rid the country of chattel slavery. In the early days of their militant thirty-year crusade they had supplemented their organization of the American Anti-Slavery Society with state and local groups. Hundreds of Northerners participated in the weekly and monthly meetings of these societies and many journeyed East each year for the annual deliberations of the national organization. Individuals and groups supported the newspapers, magazines, tracts, and pamphlets which spread abolition doctrine over the North. Both local and national societies cooperated to keep lecturers in the field. Zealous workers collected hundreds of dollars in donations to the cause and men of means who believed in the crusade supported abolition agents as well as antislavery publications.

It is, however, in the American tradition that change be accomplished through the ballot and it was to be expected that sooner or later abolition would become a political as well as a moral issue. This it did in 1840 when abolitionists divided over the question of whether to continue to center the campaign around the sinfulness of slavery or to work for the election of men who would vote the institution out of existence. Henceforth the adherents of the latter view added to the moral crusade the weight of their efforts to destroy slavery by constitutional and legalistic means. Thirty years after the establishment of the voice of the moral crusaders—William Lloyd Garrison's *Liberator*—the moralists were contending that Southerners were unfit to share the republic while the political abolitionists pressed for national action against the institution which slaveholders still claimed was subject only to state regulation. By

1861 the combined efforts of the two groups had convinced slavery's protagonists, as well as its antagonists, that only force could resolve the differences between the two sections.

Many people have aided me in the preparation of this work. My greatest debt is to Professor William B. Hesseltine of the University of Wisconsin who suggested that I study the crusading abolitionists. My deepest esteem and sincere thanks go to him for his valuable advice and inspiring encouragement throughout the development of the work. I am grateful to Miss Genevieve Winchester of the University of Wisconsin Library for the many times she has so willingly helped me, to Mr. Dallas Sweney, formerly of the Peoria Public Library, for making available to me research materials in that institution, and to Mrs. Helen Hart Metz, Elmwood, Illinois, for her work on the index. I also extend thanks to staff members of the library of the Wisconsin State Historical Society, of the University of Wisconsin Library, of the Illinois State Historical Library, Springfield, of the Bradley University Library, Peoria, Illinois, and of the Peoria Public Library.

H. C. W.

Peoria, Illinois
January 27, 1952

Contents

Illustrations

On Freedom's Altar

The Martyr In America

THE large, bristle-haired man on the platform shouted his words defiantly. His voice rang like an Old Testament trumpet. Angry men rushed down the aisles to drag him from the church. The audience rose. Sticks, stones, pieces of brick, eggs, even coins, sailed toward the pulpit.

Theodore Weld stood calm and unafraid. Receptions like this one from a Troy, New York, audience in 1836 were not new to him. He was an abolitionist and he expected to be mobbed wherever he spoke. He gloried in the persecution he suffered. "God gird us all to do valiantly for the helpless and innocent," he later wrote of the incident. "Blessed are they who die in the harness and are buried on the field or bleach there."[1] Like other abolitionists, he lovingly wore the martyr's crown of thorns. He would have died for the cause. Yet Theodore Weld was neither alone nor particularly unique in his endurance of malevolence for the freedom of the slave, for a host of nineteenth-century Americans shared the glory of persecution for the same cause

3

and through their devotion and persistence focused attention upon the crusade against America's "peculiar institution."

The nineteenth-century abolitionists, eagerly bidding for a martyr's crown, hoped to impress Americans, and to make the American heirs of the Christian tradition identify the new mode crusaders with the early martyrs of Christianity. "The blood of the martyrs," Tertullian had said, "is the seed of the church," and through the long ages the pious had revered the memory of those whose faith and persistence had endured even unto death. In tens of thousands of American homes God-fearing parents instructed children in the grim piety of their faith. In many a Protestant home, John Foxe's *Book of Martyrs* stood beside the family Bible, and Americans of all ages knew the glorious histories the English clergyman had compiled for the edification of the faithful.

Through the Reverend John Foxe's pages a thousand martyrs marched to horrible deaths. St. Stephen's blood stained Jerusalem streets as enemies dragged him away to other foes who stoned him to death. St. Peter, spent from the lash and the dungeon, expired in torment on an ignominious cross rather than again deny Jesus. St. Lawrence, beaten and bleeding, ignored the taunts of his tormentors as he roasted over a slow fire. Adalbert, Bishop of Prague, died nobly as his persecutors chained him to a post and riddled his body with poison darts. Steadfast Waldenses, their homes plundered and burned, fled to the Alps where French soldiers dashed some headlong over sheer precipices and suffocated others by firing the entrances to sheltering caves. Albigensian children died as soldiers beat out their brains before their mothers' very eyes. Under Foxe's pen, too, hundreds of lesser martyrs paraded. Some suffered terrible deaths in vats of burning lime; some, thrown to ravenous beasts, slowly expired in horrible agony. Still others endured the tortures of the rack and the stake as preliminaries to decapitation. Many screamed prayers of forgiveness for their persecutors as vinegar turned their torn and seared flesh to patches of throbbing fever; others perished as boiling pitch engulfed them.[2]

In addition to their familiarity with Foxe's martyrs, Americans saw as martyrs those who had established and developed their own United States. For early Americans had seen religious and political conflicts as intense as those of the old world. Puritan leaders like John Cotton and John Winthrop in Massachusetts desired an aristocracy of the saints. They bestowed suffrage upon Puritans only and then carefully limited church membership. In addition, Cotton mustered the power of the ministry for insistence upon the saintly magistrates' vested right to perennial election to the General Court. It was unfair, he said, to reject any officer who had maintained the sanctity of the office he held. Indeed, the leaders of the Bible Commonwealth, like those of other colonies, entered the work of freeing the New World from heresy with all the enthusiasm of medieval witch hunters.

Quakers in particular were an example of those especially dangerous to the established order. Their contention that God revealed himself to the individual through an inner light threatened the necessity for, and the power of, an interpretive clergy. Moreover, the American saints resorted to the same methods which had been applied to traditional Christian martyrs. A Massachusetts law inflicted a fine upon any shipmaster knowingly transporting Quakers to the colony. Those Quakers who slipped in suffered severe whipping and labored incommunicado in the house of correction. In 1656, two Quaker women came to Boston from Barbados. After subjecting them to the grossest indignities in a physical "examination" for evidence of witchcraft, Massachusetts authorities left them for days without food before shipping them home. Eight London Quakers shortly received similar treatment. A Boston jailer beat an arrested Quaker almost to mutilation, yet when citizens objected, a Puritan minister came to the jailer's rescue. At ministerial insistence Massachusetts dealt the death penalty to any Quaker who returned from banishment and in 1659 the authorities executed three who defied the law.[3]

Persecution, of course, did not stem nonconformity. Some men challenged the infallibility of the Puritan saints. Roger

Williams, for one, questioned that power of the churchmen over secular matters which led to persecution through civil channels for differences in religious views. So when Puritan divine John Cotton thundered against such dissenters because "if Idolators and Seducers be tolerated to seduce the servants of Christ to pollution and Apostacy, the Church will stand guilty before God of the seduction and corruption of the people of God,"[4] Williams promptly made reply. ". . . the doctrine of persecution for cause of conscience," he told the minister and those who believed with him, "is proved guilty of all the blood of the souls crying for vengeance under the altar."[5] For this and others of his heretical beliefs Williams in 1635 stood trial before the Massachusetts authorities. His doctrines were dangerous, they said, and they banished him from the colony.

The next year Mrs. Anne Hutchinson clashed with the authorities when she taught that God revealed Himself to individuals through His grace and His love. Since this doctrine directly opposed Puritan emphasis upon man's depravity in the eyes of God the judge, the churchmen summoned her to trial. Sitting as a secular court, they accused her of traducing the ministers. She had broken the fifth commandment, they decreed, for in presenting doctrines at variance with theirs she had "reproached" the fathers of the commonwealth. For her transgression the Puritan leaders ordered that she be "banished from out of our jurisdiction as being a woman unfit for our society." As she heard the sentence, Mrs. Hutchinson inquired of John Winthrop, "I desire to know wherefore I am banished." The governor's reply presaged little for the future of democratic procedures in Massachusetts. "Say no more," he said, "the court knows wherefore and is satisfied."[6]

The newer philosophy of man's freedom of judgment and his ability to make his own church and his own church government, nevertheless, persistently spread. Eventually men came to look upon Williams, Mrs. Hutchinson, and their kind as martyrs to the cause of the newer thinking. The worse their treatment, the stronger grew the feeling that they were martyrs coequal with ancient and medieval saints who suffered for adherence to a "new" Christianity and later to a "new" reform of the church.

By the third decade of the nineteenth century the martyr concept was a revered American tradition. On patriotic holidays speakers emphasized persecution as the major force which sent the first settlers to the New World. Pre-Revolution commercial and political conflicts with Great Britain revealed American colonials as martyrs to the despotism of British tyranny. The signers of the Declaration of Independence acknowledged their willingness for martyrdom when they pledged to the cause of freedom their lives, their fortunes, and their sacred honor. Patriots called Nathan Hale the "Martyr Spy" and thrilled to the words, "I only regret that I have but one life to lose for my country." Every American believed that George Washington, Robert Morris, and others made immeasurable sacrifices for the cause of liberty, and they suffered vicariously with the half-clothed, half-frozen heroes at Valley Forge. Within the memory of the generation which witnessed the abolition crusade, James Madison had urged support of the War of 1812 with the words, "With all good citizens the justice and necessity of resisting wrongs and usurpations no longer to be borne will sufficiently outweigh the privations and sacrifices inseparable from a state of war," and at the same time the newspapers spoke of flying to arms rather than submit to aggression, of suffering for glory, reputation, respect, and wisdom.[7]

Out of all this, Americans developed a concept of martyrdom which embraced certain essential ingredients. By 1830 they expected martyrs to be men who, like St. Paul, were indifferent, prior to sudden conversion, to the truth of the cause for which they later suffered. Prospective martyrs, like St. Peter, led ascetic lives either before or immediately following conversion. Martyrs prayed forgiveness for their persecutors as did St. Stephen of old. Christ's followers left families, homes, friends, and their normal labors to go with Him. Most characteristic of the martyr was his willingness, even his intense desire, to suffer persecution and death. And all, all was suffered, as by Ignatius of Antioch, who yearned for martyrdom, that their stories might move others. Moreover, by the 1830's, certain kinds of punishment had also become identified with the martyr tradition. The church martyrs had suffered stoning, scourging, boiling in oil, burning at the stake, imprisonment, dragging through the streets, abandonment to hungry wild animals.

Upon this concept the abolitionist crusaders sought to capitalize. In their own minds they identified themselves with the early proponents of the Christian faith. They magnified their sufferings, dwelt long upon their early indifference, told over and over, in trite repetition, how they first saw slavery and came under conviction of its sinfulness, how they resolved, even as the converted Saul of Tarsus, to preach the truth. They prayed for their tormentors. They abandoned their homes, as witness the lecturers of the American Anti-Slavery Society who endured inconveniences of travel and of living conditions to bring the word to antagonistic crowds. They welcomed the missiles and imprecations, the brickbats and vegetables that hostile crowds showered upon them. They found spiritual significance in tar and feathers—had not the martyrs of old been boiled in oil? They begged Americans to see the parallel between their experiences and those of Foxe's heroes and heroines.

The abolitionists' attitude came from the integration of the martyr concept with a new humanitarianism. By the first quarter of the eighteenth century American Calvinism had fallen into spiritual doldrums. The Half-way Covenant, by which the Congregational churches accepted for membership all those whose parents had belonged to the church, filled the pews with those who had never experienced the religious ecstasy of conversion. The spiritual stagnation of the churches grew worse from year to year. Then Jonathan Edwards tackled the problem. Appalled by the indifference of his Northampton, Massachusetts, congregation, he began, in the winter of 1734–1735, to revive his church. Whereas the old Calvinism had placed its emphasis on salvation only for those predestined by God, Edwards contended that the ability to receive His grace marked the elect, and he encouraged men to make personal efforts to receive God's grace.

"We should labor to be continually growing in divine love; that this may be an increasing flame in our hearts, till our hearts ascend wholly in this flame. We should be growing in obedience, and in heavenly conversation; that we may do the will of God on earth as the angels do in heaven," he said.

"What is this work or business which must be undertaken and accomplished in order to the salvation of men?" Edwards asked his listeners. Then he answered, "It is the work of seeking salvation in way of constant observance of all the duty to which God directs us in his word. If we would be saved, we must seek salvation. For although men do not obtain heaven of themselves, yet they do not go thither accidentally, or without any intention or endeavors of their own."

To those who followed this advice, the rewards were great. "And the true followers of Christ have not only ground of rest and peace of soul, by reason of their safety from evil, but on account of their sure title and certain enjoyment of all that good which they stand in need of, living, dying, and throughout all eternity. They are on a sure foundation for happiness, are built on a rock that can never be moved and have a fountain that is sufficient and can never be exhausted."[8]

Under this preaching a new fire broke out in the ranks of Calvinism. Churches grew in membership and the new enthusiasm found expression in humanitarian endeavors. Men sought to demonstrate their election in good works. At the same time, revivals swept through the middle and southern colonies. In the former, zealous Presbyterian ministers declared that outward perfection revealed inward grace. A really valid Christianity, they said, determined the believer's conduct. They urged their hearers to be about the work of their own salvation. Southern members of the same denomination flocked to sermon readings conducted by laymen and eagerly conned religious treatises and tracts collected for them in public reading rooms. Baptist preachers called for a reliance upon Christ and sent their communicants out to perform good works in His name.

Then came two English evangelists to highlight the whole revival movement. First, John Wesley preached in Georgia at the time when Edwards was electrifying Northampton. "Wheresoever therefore the gospel of Christ is preached," he said, "this his *kingdom is nigh at hand*. It is not far from every one of you. Ye may this hour enter thereinto, if so be ye hearken to his voice, 'Repent ye, and believe the Gospel.' " [9] Following Wesley, came George Whitefield. Within the year, Protestants throughout the length and breadth of the colonies hearkened to his fiery words.

"You all, my brethren, must be born again," he cried. "You must feel yourselves lost and undone in yourselves, or there is no salvation for you in the Lord Jesus Christ. . . . Do not lay the fault upon us; for the Lord now sends His servants to call and invite you to Him; and if you still refuse both him and us, what must I say?" [10]

The new thinking swept the country with the revivals which continued throughout most of the eighteenth and into the first half of the nineteenth century. The revivalists reached the common man as the established clergy had never done, the new humanitarianism as the old dogmas never had. Out of the revivalistic spirit came the abolition crusade.

Prelude
To
Crusade

OPPOSITION to American slavery came from individuals as well as from groups and was as old as the institution itself. The earliest critics condemned both the harsh treatment accorded the slave and the sinful neglect of his spiritual welfare. About 1675 Puritans John Eliot and Cotton Mather spoke out against the twin evils of slavery, and Mather published *Rules for the Society of Negroes*. Neither, however, exerted any great public effort toward emancipation. More effective as an exponent of antislavery was Samuel Sewall. Already well known as the judge who made public confession of error for his part in the witchcraft trials, Sewall wrote his *The Selling of Joseph* in 1700 when Boston was considering a law to discourage the importation of Negroes. In it he made the much quoted statement that "There is no proportion between Twenty Pieces of Silver and *Liberty*." Sixty-seven years later another Puritan, Nathaniel Appleton, added the arguments of John Locke and the natural-rights philosophers to time-honored scriptural arguments.[1]

It was the Quakers, however, rather than the Puritans, who showed the greatest antislavery zeal. In 1693 George Keith presented to the Monthly Meeting of Friends at Philadelphia a protest against slavery. Three years later he had the Yearly Meeting there adopt a resolution opposing both the importation of Negroes and the neglect of the spiritual welfare of those already here. At numerous annual meetings William Burling of Long Island warned his coreligionists of the unlawfulness of slave-keeping. In 1718 he pointed out to the elders of his church that compelling humans to serve them was inconsistent with Christian teaching. In 1729 Quaker Ralph Sandiford, Philadelphia merchant, published and circulated at his own expense an antislavery tract on *The Mystery of Iniquity*. Quaker meetings debated the righteousness of church members holding slaves. In 1790, 1794, and 1795 the Society of Friends sent to Congress petitions of protest against slavery.[2]

More effective, however, was the work of Benjamin Lay, John Woolman, Charles Osborn, and Benjamin Lundy. Each devoted a good part of his life to antislavery. In 1731 Lay, dwarfed and deformed Barbados merchant who incurred the ire of West Indian slaveholders because of his practice of giving food and religious instruction to Negro slaves, moved to the American continent and settled near Philadelphia. He annoyed Quaker meetings with persistent exhortations on the wrong of slavery. If a congregation rejected him he lay across the threshold in a driving rain, or in winter, thrust a bare leg out the meeting house door into a snow drift, excoriating protesting members with the taunt that their compassion for suffering did not extend to their poor slaves. Once he publicly pretended to stab himself to emphasize that man has in the eyes of God as much right to run his fellow creatures through with his sword as he has to keep them in bondage. In 1737 he produced the treatise *All Slave-Keepers that Keep the Innocent in Bondage, Apostates Pretending to Lay Claim to the Pure and Holy Christian Religion*. He lived to rejoice that the Philadelphia Society of Friends expelled slaveholders from membership.[3]

Less erratic than Lay's and more effective, were the labors of Woolman, Osborn, and Lundy. John Woolman began preaching against slavery in the winter of 1740–41 and taught that all people are of common descent. After a trip in 1746 through parts of Pennsylvania and Virginia he pondered the evils of a system which enslaved colored men in order to provide comfort and luxury for white masters. The result was his treatise *Some Considerations on the Keeping of Negroes,* in which he emphasized the brotherhood of man and the sinfulness of one of God's creatures holding another in bondage.

For the next twenty-two years Woolman traveled from one Quaker assembly to another through Virginia, Maryland, North Carolina, Pennsylvania, New York, Rhode Island, Massachusetts, Connecticut, and Delaware, always speaking against slavery, ever making personal calls upon slaveholders, continually serving on committees of Quakers whose purpose was to urge Friends to free their slaves.[4]

Like Woolman before him, Charles Osborn carried his antislavery message to thousands of Quakers from South Carolina to Kentucky, Indiana, Ohio, Pennsylvania, Maryland, Delaware, New York, Rhode Island, and as far north as Maine. Born in North Carolina in 1775, Osborn moved to Tennessee at the age of nineteen and entered into the work of the Society of Friends. His greatest work was with the manumission societies. In 1814 he organized the Tennessee Manumission Society "for exertions . . . to procure . . . freedom" for Negroes. Within two years he established several county societies and a state organization, all endorsing gradual emancipation. To carry his freedom message farther faster Osborn in 1817 began publication of the *Philanthropist* at Mount Pleasant, Ohio. Between 1824 and 1839 he gradually limited his efforts to improving conditions under which slaves worked; after the latter year he talked emancipation at every quarterly meeting which he attended. His thinking, however, was in advance of the Friends, for in 1842 the Indiana Yearly Meeting voted him out, along with eleven other antislavery officers. Undaunted, he helped organize the Yearly Meeting of Anti-Slavery Friends in Indiana.[5]

Carrying on Osborn's work was Benjamin Lundy who started

as agent and contributor to Osborn's *Philanthropist*. A New Jersey Quaker, born in 1789, Lundy developed an intense dislike for slave-trade operations when he worked as a saddler in Wheeling, Virginia. There he organized the Union Humane Society for the Protection of the Negro. In true Quaker fashion Lundy approached the slavery problem from the standpoint of humanitarianism, and thought in terms of what could be done to better the social and economic conditions under which the black man lived. At first he thought the solution was colonization, and made a number of trips to Texas and Mexico looking for suitable areas for resettlement. Several times he escorted recently manumitted slaves to Haiti. With the information gathered on these journeys he interested others in the cause of the Negro.

When Lundy established his antislavery *Genius of Universal Emancipation* in Ohio he published only the mildest exhortations for emancipation, yet aroused citizens drove him from place to place because of the unpopularity of his views. So with his meager equipment he migrated to Jonesboro in Tennessee, to Baltimore, to Washington, and then to Philadelphia. Working with the zeal of the crusader, Lundy traveled hundreds of miles afoot in the interest of the slave. Sometimes he carried his type and hired out as a printer in exchange for publication of his *Genius;* sometimes he walked twenty miles or more to a place of publication and then carried the completed papers on his back to return the same distance to his point of distribution. Thus he spent his strength and undermined his health.

In 1838, after a Philadelphia mob destroyed all his possessions, Lundy moved west and early in 1839 established a printing office at Lowell, Illinois, where the Putnam County Anti-Slavery Society promised to help circulate the paper. But before he could become well established in his new location, Lundy died. By his death he had completed the work which Woolman and Osborn had started, and a host of antislavery, Quaker-inspired societies remained to carry on. By the time of his death there were active organizations in New Jersey, Kentucky, New

York, Delaware, Tennessee, Ohio, North Carolina, Maryland, and Virginia.[6]

Lay, Woolman, Osborn, and Lundy were the first martyrs to the cause of freedom for the American Negro. With steady determination, each displayed the conviction and courage which Americans knew were characteristic of champions of great causes. Lay endured the ire of neighbors and of members of his church to emphasize the wrong of their slaveholding. Woolman suffered the rigors of travel to bring his antislavery message to other Quakers. Osborn saw futility in his efforts for manumission and for improved working and living conditions for slaves as Indiana Quakers rejected his antislavery philosophy. Lundy sacrificed his home and family and finally his life as the crusade for the black man consumed his entire strength. While organized groups discussed and petitioned, these four, through personal exhortation and sacrifice, linked the campaign to help the Negro with the martyr concept already developing as a great American tradition. Organized groups would continue their efforts; new conceptions of man's responsibility to God's other children would soon fire the whole antislavery movement.

Already the antislavery societies had achieved success in mitigating the evils of the peculiar institution. As early as 1795 a convention of delegates from abolition organizations had met and petitioned Congress. Then Vermont, Massachusetts, New Hampshire, Pennsylvania, Rhode Island, Connecticut, New York, and New Jersey, had passed laws outlawing slavery within their limits. In addition, Congress had forbidden slavery in the Northwest Territory and had set 1808 as the date for the prohibition of further importation of slaves. The foundations for a concerted move against slavery were already laid.

While the revivalists were intensifying and spreading the new religious thinking which emphasized the individual's personal responsibility for his own salvation and were encouraging men to manifest evidence of soul-saving efforts, many Americans were accepting the socio-political ideas of the European natural-rights philosophers. These thinkers also emphasized the importance of the individual but stressed his responsibility for the difference between the ideal and the real conditions under which human beings exist in this world. As early as 1767 another immigrant Quaker, Anthony Benezet, moved from France to the neighborhood of Philadelphia. He published the essay *A Caution to Great Britain and Her Colonies, in a Short Representation of the Calamitous State of the Enslaved Negroes in the British Dominion.* Revealing the influence of the natural rights philosophers, he said in part: "Upon the whole . . . it must appear to every honest, unprejudiced Reader, that the Negroes are equally entitled to the Common Priviledges of Mankind with the Whites, that they have the same rational Powers; the same natural Affections, and are as susceptible of Pain and Grief as they, that therefore the bringing and Keeping them in Bondage is an Instance of Oppression and Injustice of most grievous Nature, such as scarcely to be paralleled by an Example in the present or former Ages."[7] The crusade against slavery was a result of the combination of the revivalist-taught personal responsibility for salvation and the natural-rights humanitarianism.

Prophet of this broadened Christianity was Charles Grandison Finney, western New York lawyer who forsook the law to study the Bible. Finney termed God's all-encompassing goodness His benevolence; benevolence he explained as "willing the existence of the highest attainable good." To attain accord with God's benevolence the individual must desire the highest possible good, not in order to promote his own selfish interests, but to glorify God and increase His happiness.

"Benevolence is good will," declared Finney. "Benevolence to God, is preferring His happiness and glory to all created good. Benevolence to men is the exercise of the same regard to, and desire for their happiness, as we have for our own. . . . Perfect benevolence to God and man, would at once give us a share in all the happiness of earth and heaven. . . . If we desire the happiness of others, their happiness will increase our own, according to the strength of our desire. If we desire their welfare as much as we do our own, we are made as happy by good, known to be

Above: Portrait of Prudence Crandall painted at the request of the New England Anti-Slavery Society after Connecticut citizens forced her to abandon her school for Negro girls. Sale of the portrait helped to spread the abolitionist gospel. *Below:* Anthony Benezet, a Quaker who worked to improve the Negro's lot.

Only three or four different headings were used on Garrison's *Liberator* in the course of its existence from January 1, 1831 to January 1, 1866. This one of April 9, 1858 is more elaborate than the earlier headings. The first ones showed only the slave auction scene at the left above. Later Garrison added to this to make an even more melodramatic heading.

conferred on them, as upon ourselves; and nothing but selfishness prevents our tasting the cup of every man's happiness, and sharing equally with him in all his joys.

"Selfishness is the discord of the soul. It is the jarring, and dissonance, and grating, of hell's eternal anguish. Benevolence, on the other hand, is the melody of the soul. . . . To be happy, then, you must be benevolent.

"Look at the consequence of your present course, to yourself, your friends over whom you have influence, to the church, and to the world. Will you continue to cast firebrands, arrows, and death—to throw all your influence, your time and talents, your body and soul, into the scale of selfishness? Shall all your influence continue to be upon the wrong side, to increase the wickedness and misery of earth, to gratify the devil and grieve the Son of God!"[8]

In 1824 Finney began his ministry in western New York. As had other evangelists before him, he stood aghast that people could hear the message of the Gospel and remain utterly unmoved to love of either God or man. He strove, therefore, to break down indifference. Standing erect to his full six feet, two inches of height, Finney appraised his audiences and preached directly at the shortcomings of the sinners before him. His booming voice reached all; his logic moved many. When members showed signs of conviction of sin, Finney or one of his "Holy Band" of assistants went amongst them, quietly consoled each, and urged prayer as the means to God's grace and the will to achieve benevolence. From his revivals men went forth to glorify their God through justice and mercy to His creatures.

Although Finney's opposition to slavery was but a part of his over-all philosophy that the godly man must eschew selfishness for benevolence, Finneyism was a potent ingredient of American abolitionism. In the light of the great revivalist's teachings, a large number of his converts quickly saw American chattel slavery as a terrible transgression. Deep under the conviction of sin, they were willing adherents to the movement which William Lloyd Garrison would soon launch.

Hear
Ye
The
Prophet!

BUT other forces than Finney revivalism with its emphasis upon benevolence were helping to mould the abolition crusade. Out of New England there came a man who saw slavery as a national sin and who, like John the Baptist, called upon a nation to repent. William Lloyd Garrison fearlessly faced a martyr's crown. To Garrison abolition was a godsend, a crusade worthy of his ambition and talent. Born in 1805 in Newburyport, Massachusetts, he was taught by a pious mother to see moral implications in all things. He spent a troubled childhood and youth shuttling from one occupation to another, dissatisfied with all. Then in 1819 he found the printer's trade. Here was an honorable vocation, fraught with possibilities for a young man of piety and a knack with words. His first anonymous contributions brought praise-filled letters to the paper. Garrison had launched his career.

But a crusader must have a crusade, and Garrison tried them all. He excoriated the Holy Alliance and beat the drums for

Greek independence. Three years after he finished his printer's apprenticeship, he became coeditor and publisher of a temperance paper, the *National Philanthropist*. Later the same year, at Bennington, Vermont, as editor of a John Quincy Adams-for-president paper, Garrison agitated for world peace, Clay's American System, and the extension of popular and practical education. But for a knight in search of wrongs to right, none of these had sufficient popular appeal.

Then Garrison stumbled upon antislavery. At first his stand on the new issue was groping and confused. He begged the readers of his Adams paper, *The Journal of the Times*, to petition Congress for the abolition of slavery in the District of Columbia. On July 4, 1828, he spoke in Boston in praise of the American Colonization Society! Garrison had found his life work. He knew he wanted a cause; he had a certain facility with words; he had a mania for uniqueness and for attention. If, somehow, he could take over the now temperate antislavery movement he would have a crusade worthy of his ambition and talent.

Gentle, soft-spoken Quaker Benjamin Lundy became the means of Garrison's full-fledged entrance into the abolition movement. Impressed with the young editor's antislavery articles in the Bennington paper, Lundy walked from Baltimore to the Vermont town to urge Garrison to join him in the work of publishing the *Genius*. So Garrison went to Baltimore and the call to martyrdom was loud in his ear.

About three years before, a notoriously cruel slave trader, one Austin Woolfolk, had beaten Lundy mercilessly in the streets of Baltimore for his stand against slavery. Now, shortly after Garrison joined Lundy, he heard that Woolfolk resented the young writer's criticism of the slavery policy of another paper. In the next *Genius* Garrison challenged him to appear in person for a debate. Woolfolk never came, but Garrison had his cue. The way was clear. A crusader must do some challenging. On November 13, 1829, he published a brief note under the heading *Domestic Slave Trade* in which he said: "Scarcely a vessel, perhaps, leaves this port for New Orleans without carrying off in chains large numbers of the unfortunate blacks. The ship *Francis*, Brown, which sailed hence a few weeks since, transported *seventy-five*. This vessel hails from my native place (Newburyport, Mass.), and belongs to *Francis Todd*.—So much for New England principle!"[1] The next week he reiterated the story. The charge was true, but the young crusader did not limit his accusation to the one cargo and Todd triumphantly had him convicted for libel. The sentence was a term in the Baltimore jail; the reward was martyrdom of a sort.

From the jail the young crusader wrote, ". . . here I strut, the lion of the day; and, of course, attract a great number of visitors, as the exhibition is gratuitous. . . ."[2] To make sure of wide recognition he scored Todd in a newspaper notice, notified the *Boston Courier* of his detention, and enclosed a sonnet to the sleep which he did not get in jail. When the editor of the *Newburyport Herald* questioned the wisdom of his actions, Garrison wrote him a three-column letter. In addition, he penned and published an eight-page pamphlet, *A Brief Sketch of the Trial of William Lloyd Garrison, for an Alleged Libel on Francis Todd, of Massachusetts*. But his imprisonment had another important result. Arthur Tappan, New York silk merchant, who, with his brother Lewis, spent much of the profit of the business on reform, heard of Garrison and his cause. He bailed him out.

Garrison made his initial martyrdom count. He started immediately on a lecture tour which included Philadelphia, New York, New Haven, Hartford, and his native Newburyport. How glorious it was when church trustees in Boston closed doors to him! There was fame and fortune in this business of abolition and Garrison proceeded to make the most of it. He proudly announced that the only hall open to him was Abner Kneeland's Julien Hall—"hall of the infidels" Boston called it. At the same time he wrote to prominent men, Daniel Webster and William Ellery Channing among them, and asked them to save the country from slavery.[3] In 1830 Garrison announced that he would shortly publish his own paper in the national capital.

When he started the *Liberator*, however, it was in Boston, where he and a partner, Isaac Knapp, worked as journeymen in exchange for the use of another paper's type in printing it. But Garrison had planned wisely. The fiery bannerhead of his first issue, "Our Country is the World—Our Countrymen are all Mankind," as well as his flaming promise, "I am in earnest—I will not equivocate—I will not excuse—I will not retreat a single inch—AND I WILL BE HEARD," brought in financial support from old Massachusetts antislavery men, and Garrison had a good start. The *Liberator* was from the first the trumpet of aroused abolitionism. The vituperative editor battled the Colonization Society and every antislavery speaker or writer who differed a hair's breadth from him. He appealed to the free Negroes for support, and through it all built himself up as the champion of and martyr to the cause of the suffering slave.

"Foes are on my right hand and on my left. The tongue of detraction is busy against me," he wrote to certain Negroes who sent him money. Again he penned: "In attacking the system of slavery, I clearly foresaw all that has happened to me. I knew at the commencement that my motives would be impeached, my warnings ridiculed, my person persecuted, my sanity doubted, my life jeoparded; but the clank of the prisoner's chains broke upon my ear—it entered deeply into my soul—I looked up to Heaven for strength to sustain me in the perilous work of emancipation, and my resolution was taken. Thanks be to God, that resolution grows loftier with time, and sinks its base deeper and broader as danger approximates."[4]

Meanwhile, Finneyism had overflowed into abolitionism. After his term as a member of the "Holy Band," Theodore Weld had continued his education at Oneida Institute at Whitesborough, New York. There Charles Stuart, British emancipationist, paid his expenses. For two years, from 1829 to 1831, Stuart peppered Weld with antislavery literature from England

and begged him to take the platform for the abolition of American slavery. Weld finally acceded and shortly found the means for drawing some vital support to the antislavery crusade.

One result of the breakdown of Calvinism and the upsurge of humanitarianism had been the formation, between 1820 and 1830, of the "benevolent societies" to foster reform: temperance, world peace, the salvation of sailors, Sabbath observance, and public education. By the latter year there were eight large organizations, mostly modeled after British examples. Supporting these was a comparatively small group of wealthy men, amongst whom were Arthur and Lewis Tappan. The latter Weld had once characterized as a glorious fellow, conscientious and intelligent, with as much moral courage as John Knox. "If he gets fairly combustionized he will burn all before him," Weld had concluded.[5] The Tappans heard Finney in New York and immediately added Finneyism to their long list of philanthropies. They established the *Evangelist* in New York so that Finney could carry his exhortation to greater numbers. In July, 1831, Weld drew the Tappans into the antislavery movement when he attended a New York meeting of the Association of Gentlemen, the wealthy backers of the benevolent societies. The Tappans customarily dominated the projects they supported.

Their domination of the antislavery movement, however, met an obstacle in Boston's crusading young editor. By 1833 William Lloyd Garrison was well into the work of dominating the antislavery movement. He needed prestige, however, and in that year planned to get it. Hence when the New England Anti-Slavery Society decided to send an agent to Britain to obtain aid for the American abolition crusade, Garrison maneuvered his own appointment and managed to get from it much publicity and prestige. To the quarterly meeting of the society at Boston he said that the chances of his ever again addressing them depended upon God's handling of the Atlantic winds. "Whatever may be the event with me," he said, "see to it that you grow not weary in well doing. . . . Suffer no discouragement to depress, no obstacle to hinder, no persecution to deter, no power to awe, no opposition to defeat you in your great and glorious enterprise."[6] He delivered farewell addresses to as many groups as would listen. He told a colored audience that national attention to the antislavery crusade was the result of the truth-spreading of the *Liberator*. He was, he said, keeping just ahead of a sheriff who wanted to arrest him for his speeches. Despite this, he took time to sit for a portrait so that prints of the Negro's true friend could be distributed while he was in England. From New York he wrote that he would have to sneak aboard the Liverpool packet to avoid enemies who would kidnap him for the Georgia reward upon his head. "My friends are full of apprehension and disquietude; but I *cannot* know fear. I feel that it is impossible for danger to awe me. I tremble at nothing but my own delinquencies, as one who is bound to be perfect, even as my heavenly Father is perfect."[7]

In England William Lloyd Garrison managed to meet all the great names of English abolitionism; he spared no pains to make sure that Americans heard about it. He gloated that Thomas F. Buxton, English emancipationist, believed him a Negro, "For Mr. Buxton had somehow or other supposed that no white American could plead for those in bondage as I had done, and therefore I must be black!"[8] Speaking to an English audience in Exeter Hall on July 13, 1833, he said: "It would neither be modest nor proper for me, on this occasion, to make a parade of the sacrifices of time, of money, of health, or of labor, I have made, nor of the perils I have risked, or the persecution encountered, or the sufferings endured, since I first stood forth as the advocate of my enslaved countrymen. . . ."[9]

But Garrison's great triumph in England came a month before he was to sail for home. On July 26 the famed William Wilberforce died and William Lloyd Garrison walked with the English abolitionist George Thompson behind a long line of dignitaries for the funeral at Westminster. How impressive that story would look in the *Liberator!*

Garrison was hopeful that his return to New York would encourage further persecution. Actually his arrival was peaceful.

Yet because a mob opposed a New York City Anti-Slavery Society organization meeting which convened some four days after his arrival, Garrison wrote later: "It has been the most eventful year in my history. I have been the occasion of many uproars, and a continual disturber of the public peace. As soon as I landed, I turned the city of New York upside down. Five thousand people turned out to see me tarred and feathered, but were disappointed. There was also a hubbub in Boston on my arrival."[10] At the same time he took credit for the call to organize a national antislavery society at Philadelphia in late 1833. Still operating on the principle that potential martyrs must start their own fights, he attacked the New York papers which he said inspired mobs against him and he said in verse,

> Glory, to them, who die in this great cause!
> *Mobs—judges*—can inflict no brand of shame,
> Or shape of death, to shroud them from applause!
> No! manglers of the martyr's earthly frame,
> Your hangmen fingers cannot touch his fame.
> Still in this guilty land there shall be some
> Proud hearts—the shrine of Freedom's vestal flame;
> Long trains of ill may pass unheeded—dumb—
> But Vengeance is behind, and Justice is to come![11]

At the organization meeting of the American Anti-Slavery Society at Philadelphia in December, 1833, Garrison forced the adoption of a Declaration of Sentiments which endorsed immediate emancipation for the Negro. Lewis Tappan presented a public eulogy when he addressed the meeting, "Sir, we should throw the shield of our protection and esteem around Mr. Garrison. . . . And, sir, there must be martyrs in this cause."[12]

Garrison pushed ahead with his dominance in the movement. In September, 1834, the English abolitionist George Thompson arrived in New York for a lecture tour of the New England states. Newspapers at once excoriated him and some feared for his safety. Abolitionists rejoiced in his persecution as audiences received him ungraciously. Garrison himself opened a new *Liberator* column, "The Refuge of Oppression," and declared that abolitionists were suffering persecution akin to that of the Christian martyrs.

Later Garrison wrote: "That some of us will be assassinated or abducted, seems more than probable. . . . There is a whole eternity of consolation in this assurance—he who loses his life for Christ's sake shall find it." Indeed, Angelina Grimké was thinking right with him when she had said, "A *hope* gleams across my mind, that *our* blood will be spilt, instead of the slaveholders'; *our* lives will be taken, and theirs spared." When his enemies erected a gallows before his house, Garrison told his *Liberator* readers, "To the obedient death is no calamity. If we perish, our loss will but hasten the destruction of slavery more certainly."[13]

Persecution was rampant in Boston. On October 21, 1835, a postponed meeting of the Female Anti-Slavery Society convened at the rooms of the state society in the *Liberator* neighborhood. The audience, restricted to women, expected to hear George Thompson. For weeks previously Garrison had been screaming through his newspaper columns that other papers were purposely linking his name with Thompson's in an attempt to arouse a mob against both of them. Indeed, there was so much excitement and so many rumors told of planned riot that Thompson left town long before the appointed assembly.

But the meeting must go ahead; the women were already gathering. Garrison stepped into the breach to deliver them a talk. A little before the start of the meeting, he found a large crowd blocking the doors. He explained that Thompson had fled and advised them to break up. They would not heed; they became bolder and more vociferous. Garrison made his way up the stairs to the second-floor room where the meeting was about to open. He begged those who crowded the upper steps and were edging into the room to break up the meeting, to leave, but they only became more boisterous. Then he remembered that his presence would make matters worse for the anti-slavery women; he heard them voice their concern for his safety. So, accompanied by fellow abolitionist Charles C. Burleigh,[14] Garrison slipped across the hall to the office maintained by the state society for the distribution of antislavery tracts and pamphlets. There he sat down to write to a friend an account of the drama he was witnessing. Burleigh locked the door as the mob outside howled for Thompson. From across the hall both men could hear the voice of Mayor Theodore Lyman[15] as he appeared to assure the rioters that the English agitator had departed. They heard the crowd hoot and jeer as men tried unsuccessfully to break down the partition which separated the jammed hall from the meeting room where the Female Anti-Slavery Society continued its session.

Then the mob found Garrison. Smashing the lower panel of the door to the room where he sat, the leaders peered in at him. "There he is! That's Garrison!" they shouted. "Out with the scoundrel!"[16] The editor of the *Liberator* moved quickly. As the cry grew louder he dashed out the rear door of the room to another part of the building, dropped from a window to a low shed, and ran through a carpenter shop which faced another street. But the mob was upon his heels. To leave the shop would be to run directly into their arms. This Garrison offered to do, but Burleigh would not hear of it and hustled him to a hiding place in an upstairs room. But the rioters followed, and Garrison shortly found himself held before an open window some feet above the ground, in the firm grip of riot leaders.

Some men jeered; some clamored that he not be killed outright. But Garrison bowed to the mob and calmly agreed to surrender. So, after those closest had coiled a rope around his body, he went willingly down the ladder.

"I was thus conducted through Wilson's Lane into State Street, in the rear of the City Hall, over the ground that was stained with the blood of the first martyrs in the cause of LIBERTY AND INDEPENDENCE by the memorable massacre of 1770. . . ."[17] An observer noted that coatless, hatless, and afraid to wear his glasses though he was, William Lloyd Garrison walked along "erect and calm, like a martyr going to the stake."

To the City Hall they marched him. "To the Frog Pond

with him," shouted many. But someone shoved him into the building and in a moment he was upstairs awaiting the mayor who had gone to the second floor, climbed out to stand upon a capstone above the main door, and was making a last appeal to the mob to disperse.

When Mayor Lyman returned, he and his civil advisers thought it safest to commit Garrison to jail for "disturbing the peace." So they hustled him into one of the two hacks which had been brought to different doors to divert the mob and off to jail went Garrison. The mobsters dashed in pursuit of the carriage. Some tried to drag him from the vehicle; some clung to the wheels; some yanked and pulled to open the doors; some seized the bridles and others tried to upset the carriage. None succeeded; for the second time Garrison went to jail for his antislavery activities.

Here was martyrdom. Upon the walls of his cell Garrison wrote, "Wm. Lloyd Garrison was put into this cell on Wednesday afternoon, October 21, 1835, to save him from the violence of a 'respectable and influential' mob, who sought to destroy him for preaching the abominable and dangerous doctrine, that 'all men are created equal,' and that all oppression is odious in the sight of God. 'Hail, Columbia!' Cheers for the Autocrat of Russia and the Sultan of Turkey!

"Reader, let this inscription remain till the last slave in this despotic land be loosed from his fetters."[18]

Upon his release the following day, Garrison, with his wife, left immediately for a visit with her family in Connecticut. His brother-in-law arranged to circulate the Boston mob story and Garrison wrote to his friends of his "escape out of the jaws of the lion." The abolitionists knew reaction to martyrdom would favor the abolition cause. The *Liberator* made the most of the story.

By 1836 an open rift existed among American abolitionists. At the center of it was Garrison, to many the very embodiment of the abolition spirit. But to some his enthusiasm for reform was running away with him, and they complained bitterly of his faults. Lewis Tappan confided to a friend that Garrison's continued argument in the *Liberator* over proper Sabbath-keeping was a "germ of animosity and contention among the brethren."[19]

Then in 1837 certain leaders of organized religion in Massachusetts began to criticize many of Garrison's ideas. In July of that year, in a *Pastoral Letter of the General Association of Massachusetts to the Orthodox Congregational Churches,* the clergymen declared that perplexing subjects should not be forced upon any church for debate and that outsiders had no business coming into the congregations of settled ministers to preach on these subjects. Furthermore, to encourage women to speak in public meetings and to appear on the lecture platform threatened the female character with widespread and permanent injury. Garrison fought back through the *Liberator* columns, but his fury only called out more opposition. A group of New England clergymen now joined in an *Appeal of Clerical Abolitionists on Anti-Slavery Measures.* In this and in a subsequent *Appeal* from abolitionists of the Andover Theological Seminary, the clerics declared their deep grief over Garrison's damaging remarks about both Gospel ministers and the American Board of Foreign Missions, over unsettling discussions in the churches, over public antislavery lectures by women, and over Henry C. Wright's antislavery discourses for children.[20] The more Garrison fought back in the *Liberator,* the more savage became the attacks in the various religious magazines. Shortly the editors of the *Christian Mirror,* the *Vermont Chronicle,* the *New York Evangelist,* and the *New York Observer* all voiced opposition to Garrison. They maintained that since Garrison insisted upon dragging into an antislavery paper extraneous matters like women's rights, world peace, Sabbath-keeping, temperance, and the like in language too vituperative to be Christian, the movement needed a new society and a new paper. Furthermore, they said, many people thought the Massachusetts Anti-Slavery Society controlled the *Liberator's* editorial policy because that organization had assumed responsibility for printing and publishing the paper and they blamed the society for Garrison's extremes.

Garrison fumed and determined to hold his own. He counted heavily on support from the Executive Committee of the American Anti-Slavery Society in New York. His righteous indignation flared when Lewis Tappan wrote him that the committee was remaining silent, not because the members approved of the *Appeal,* but because they could not deny all the charges made against the *Liberator* and its editor. Garrison had been wrong to single out two visiting clergymen as slaveholders; his Sabbath observance discussion, his expression of his peculiar doctrines on national and family government were injudicious. Indeed, his editorials were not always kind and Christian. Furthermore, said the New York philanthropist, Garrison's great concern over the *Appeal* indicated a lack of confidence in himself. He should have asked everyone to overlook the document, forget personalities, and devote all energy to the cause. That policy, attended by a correction of the *Liberator's* real faults along the lines mentioned, would cut the ground from under the appellants' arguments.

Garrison fumed again. The Committee's refusal to make any public statement in his defense, he wrote a relative, was actually criminal. Nor did advice similar to Tappan's from his old friends Elizur Wright and William Goodell,[21] change his mind. He would proceed according to his own infallible conscience. He announced that at the end of the year he would resume full financial responsibility for the *Liberator* and the state society would no longer have to make apologies for the truth of his strictures. As the year 1837 closed, he boldly announced that henceforth the paper would discuss not only antislavery, but also would devote a little more space to world peace and women's rights.

Early in 1839 Garrison learned that Charles T. Torrey, spokesman for certain ministers in Massachusetts, was urging antislavery meetings throughout the state to replace the *Liberator* with a new paper which would not discuss extraneous matters like women's rights, Sabbath-keeping, world peace, and nonresistance. William Lloyd Garrison suddenly saw persecution by his fellow abolitionists replacing that of mobite public opinion. "For, by 'hanging Garrison' and repudiating the *Liberator,* they will surely condescend to take the reins of antislavery management into their own hands! . . . No attempt is to be made to lower down the standard—O no!—but simply to change the men to whom has been entrusted the management of the enterprise, and put in their place younger men, better men, who will accomplish wonders, and perform their duties more faithfully—that's all!" he wrote editorially on January 11, 1839.[22] Indeed, the dispute between the Massachusetts Anti-Slavery Society Board of Managers and the American Anti-Slavery Society Executive Committee over the method of collecting funds, the decision of his clerical opponents to publish the *Massachusetts Abolitionist* to make up for the *Liberator's* preoccupation with other reforms, and the insistence of certain abolitionists that the crusade be made political, convinced Garrison that his enemies were determined to wreck the movement whose champion he was. "I anticipate a breaking up of our whole organization," he wrote. "But my mind is calm and peaceful. The Lord of hosts is my rock and refuge."[23]

But Garrison determined to save the movement from his enemies if he could. At the annual meeting of the Massachusetts society in early May he had more support than his opponents. Late the same month, however, they bolted the New England Convention of Abolitionists and established the Massachusetts Abolition Society. In July, the five hundred delegates to the National Convention of Abolitionists at Albany, called by the New York Anti-Slavery Society Executive Committee and approved by the national society, voted down his resolutions against abolitionists nominating candidates for president and vice-president of the United States. In another year the American Anti-Slavery Society was practically extinct and the anti-Garrison men formed a new organization and supported the Liberty Party in the hope of ending slavery through political means.

But William Lloyd Garrison held that the move to free the Negro was a moral, rather than a political, crusade. Moreover, his recognition of abolition as the cardinal issue did not blind him to the urgency of other problems of humanitarianism and reform. When, therefore, the political abolitionists in 1840 formed the Liberty Party, Garrison broke completely with them. He continued the moral crusade with emphasis upon the sin of slavery and accompanied it with constant agitation for all the reforms which his opponents considered extraneous matters. In August, 1840, he attended the World's Anti-Slavery Convention in London, but refused to participate in the deliberations of a body which denied membership to women delegates. His characterization of his actions there—he emphasized his attitude by becoming merely a gallery spectator—revealed as well his conception of his significance to abolition and other phases of humanitarianism. "In short," he wrote from London, "I did what I could for the redemption of the human race."[24]

In the years after 1840 William Lloyd Garrison eschewed political abolitionism and fought both the sin of slaveholding and the rashness of those who had wrecked the moral crusade whose champion and martyr he was. Meanwhile, the martyr concept had become integrated with abolitionism and other men suffered for the cause of the poor slave.

The
First
Martyr

BY THE third decade of the nineteenth century two great, deep-seated American traditions had united to produce the abolition movement. The one was the natural-rights philosophy with its egalitarian and humanitarian implications, the other was the Christian doctrine of salvation through personal effort which had been preached by Jonathan Edwards, had been given direction by the Quaker organizations, and had been revitalized by Finney's insistence upon the necessity for benevolence. But, as Garrison realized, one essential ingredient which these two traditions had in common was the blood of the martyrs. Abolitionism yet lacked martyrs and it was yet to be demonstrated that men could become so devoted to the rights of the slave that they would sacrifice their lives on the altars of the Negro's freedom. As William Ellery Channing testified in 1836, "One kidnaped, murdered abolitionist, would do more for the violent destruction of slavery than a thousand societies."[1] Then in 1837 abolitionism claimed its first martyr. Thereafter the blood of Elijah Lovejoy cried out from the Alton flagstones to the consciences of men.

In the fall of 1827 Elijah Parish Lovejoy arrived in St. Louis.

Son of a New England Congregational minister, Lovejoy at the age of twenty-five had behind him a brilliant college career at Waterville, Maine, and was looking for worlds to conquer. He tried school teaching and he tried publishing a political news-paper. Neither occupation satisfied him. Then he found the current militant evangelism.

The revival spirit was sweeping the country. Evangelists held protracted meetings everywhere and called upon Americans to hear the voice of the Lord. In January, 1832, Lovejoy wrote his parents: "I attended the inquiry meetings, and for some time really felt a delight in religious exercises. . . . I have reason to hope that the good spirit has again visited me, inviting me to forsake the world and come to Jesus. . . . And now, my dear and honored Father and Mother, will you not pray for me—if possible, with more earnestness than you have ever yet done?" His parents rejoiced that the Lord had answered their prayers, when, in February, 1832, the son penned, "When this letter reaches you, I shall, if God spares my life and health, be on my way to Princeton, in New Jersey, for the purpose of enter-ing upon my studies preparatory to the work of the ministry. . . . I was, by divine grace, enabled to bring all my sins and all my sorrows, and lay them at the feet of Jesus, and to receive the blessed assurance that He had accepted me, all sinful and pol-luted as I was."[2] For the next year Elijah Lovejoy worked dili-gently and prayed faithfully in anticipation of a life in the kind of God-service urged by the revivalists. In April, 1833, the Second Presbytery of Philadelphia licensed him to preach and he accepted assignments in Newport, Rhode Island, and then in the Spring Street Church in New York City.

But eastern pastorates, sedate and spiritless, could not satisfy Lovejoy's burning enthusiasm for the cause of the Lord. His Christian zeal combined with the call to fierce and heady exist-ence attuned his spirit to the frontier. In less than six months the youthful minister harkened to a call from his earlier haunts in St. Louis. There a group of friends, admirers of his daring, and quoters, like him, of pure Protestant dogma, raised funds for a press and plant to publish a vigorous anti-Catholic news-paper and called Lovejoy to be its editor. He accepted the call, hurried to St. Louis, and quickly brought out the first issue of the *Observer*.

The new editor brought only zeal and energy to the Protestant cause. His editorials repeated the labored arguments against Catholic dogmas, and his news columns carried only the trite stories of Romish corruption. He did not like the doctrine of transubstantiation, or sin-secreting convents, or Catholics in general or Irish Catholics in particular. His attacks upon these ancient themes had heat but not light. He gave no new reasons for his venom. When the Catholics accorded him an undue respect and discussed him in his own terms, Lovejoy exulted in his persecution.[3]

Perhaps it all whetted his appetite for vituperation. Or perhaps he grew weary of the endless round of theological disputation. Or he may have remembered the humanitarianism of the revivalists' philosophy. Whatever the reasons—and they were hidden deep in the zealot's psyche—Lovejoy began to give attention to the new crusade the abolitionists were waging.

At first, as abolitionist agitators appeared in the Missouri town and as their arguments crept into religious journalism, Lovejoy vacillated and floundered amid current concepts of slavery. He could accept readily enough the revivalist doctrine that slavery was a sin. But, from the vantage point of slave-holding St. Louis, where there still were memories of the controversy over Missouri's admission to the union, Lovejoy could see that immediate emancipation would create more problems than it would solve. In the editorials which he interspersed among his assaults upon the Roman hierarchy he explained the slave question with more than his usual caution. He approved, he said, of the Lane debates. He believed the public conscience should arouse itself against the sin of slavery. Yet he saw the Negro as fit only for Africa, and solemnly approved the efforts of the American Colonization Society.

But so temperate a program could not long contain Lovejoy's

crusading impulse. During 1835, while a constitutional convention debated slavery's status in Missouri, he took his stand. "Gradual emancipation," he said in the *Observer,* "is the remedy we propose."[4] He demanded, with the same fire that he demanded that Irishmen give up the Pope, that his adopted state immediately formulate emancipation plans.

When the way was clear, Lovejoy knew only how to advance. Soon he was speaking at church meetings, repeating the abolitionist sermons against sin and calling slaveholders to repentance. And soon, too, he began to learn of the reaction. An elder of St. Louis's First Presbyterian Church warned the prophetic Elijah that there were ugly mumblings that mobs would assemble. In September, Lovejoy went to a camp meeting sixty miles away. There he heard that two men who planned to assault him had gone to a nearby village to search for him. When they did not find him, he rejoiced that the Lord protected him. Shortly thereafter, the *Observer's* editor journeyed to Union, Missouri, to aid in preparations for a forthcoming synod meeting at Marion. With him he carried antislavery resolutions to present to the church. When the synod met the issue was joined. An elder from St. Louis, opposing Lovejoy, demanded that the Presbyterian body disavow abolitionism. The church, said the elder, must certainly be destroyed by abolitionist rantings, and the synod agreed.

Thereafter, citizens of St. Louis brought pressure upon Lovejoy. A number of them wrote demanding that, in the future, he "pass over in silence everything connected with the subject of Slavery." The public mind, they explained, was already too greatly excited over the "unjustifiable interference of our northern brethren with our social relations" to endure sound doctrine on the subject of slavery.[5] A public meeting deplored the interference of "foreign emissaries" with the slavery problem and condemned abolition activity as dangerous to the union. A vigilance committee prepared to investigate citizens suspected of abolitionism.

During most of October Lovejoy was absent from St. Louis,

attending church meetings, and *Observer* backers kept the slavery question out of the paper. They feared the mobs which daily threatened its office. To the absent editor friends sent messages that return to St. Louis during the current state of the public mind was to court disaster. But Elijah Lovejoy had the courage as well as the zeal of the prophet. With his pious wife he solemnly agreed that where duty called, the brave must follow. He went back to St. Louis.

There his zealot heart thrilled to the danger of the city's turmoil over the recent whipping, by "respectable citizens," of two men accused of aiding Negroes to free states. Lovejoy girded for a fight as a city newspaper proclaimed him an abolitionist, the elder who had opposed his antislavery resolutions at synod called his attitude dangerous, and a committee of St. Louisans demanded a change in the conduct of the *Observer*. To his family in Maine he confided that he expected to be lynched, tarred and feathered, even hanged. ". . . I will not run," he concluded, "until I have been whipped as often, at least, as Paul was—eight times. . . . And let me entreat my brothers and sisters to pray for me; that I may pass through this 'fiery trial,' without denying my Lord and Master."[6]

Lovejoy publicly disavowed immediatism but declared that he had never promised to forego discussion of slavery. To the published resolutions of a public meeting which convened to consider the course currently pursued by antislavery men, he addressed a detailed answer. Refuting the charge that he had secretly sent copies of the *Emancipator* into Missouri, he nonetheless defended his right to send if he desired. But, he said, he would always send openly. No mob could tell a free citizen what to think or what to print.

Those of Lovejoy's friends who actively supported the *Observer* were not so sure of the wisdom of his course. They feared that his policy endangered their property, and in the fall of 1835 asked him to retire as editor. He agreed that their request was fair, in view of public opinion in St. Louis and his own determination to serve conscience only. He signed a note for the final five hundred dollars of his obligation for the financial support of the *Observer* and prepared to leave St. Louis. But as he gathered up his few belongings for a new start across the river in the free state of Illinois, the holder of his note announced his willingness to risk five hundred dollars to keep the *Observer* in St. Louis. In great relief and exultation Lovejoy took the cancelled note and went back to his newspaper. For some months he lived and worked quietly in St. Louis.

Then in May, 1836, a mob broke into the city jail, removed a mulatto who had murdered a white man, chained him to a tree and burned him alive, even refusing his request that they shoot him to end his agony. Lovejoy wept as he wrote full details of the story; he trembled in righteous fury as he editorially flayed other Missouri editors who ignored it. When Judge Luke Lawless, hearing the case against the indicted mobsters, charged the jury to remember that the acts of mobs are beyond the reach of human law, Lovejoy raged in indignation. It would be, he wrote, "better that editor, printer, and publishers, should be chained to the same tree as the mulatto M'Intosh, and share his fate, than that the doctrines promulgated by Judge Lawless, from the bench, should become prevalent in this community."[7] He would expect nothing better, he concluded, for Lawless as both immigrant and Catholic could neither understand nor appreciate fundamental American principles.

But despite his courageous stand, Lovejoy had decided to quit St. Louis. At the height of popular tension over the McIntosh case he announced that he was removing immediately to Alton, Illinois, where he would continue publication of the *Observer*. But before he could move, a St. Louis mob entered the newspaper office and threw much of his office equipment into the Mississippi. He salvaged what he could and departed with his family for Alton. But again misfortune trailed him. His press arrived on Sunday when there was no one to receive it. Before workers could get to it an Alton mob toppled it into the river. Lovejoy wrote his family in Maine: "Why, when my services are so much needed, I should be laid up on a bed of sickness,

I cannot tell; why, when God has in his wise and holy providence let loose upon me angry, and wicked men, He would also
so heavily lay his hand upon me, I cannot see, but he can, and I
desire to submit without a murmur. . . . I have opened my
mouth for the dumb, I have plead the cause of the poor and
oppressed—I have maintained the rights of humanity, and of
nature outraged in the person of my fellow-men around me, and
I have done it, as is my nature, openly, boldly, and in the face
of day, and for these things I am brot into these straits. For
these things I have seen my family scattered, my office broken
up, my furniture—as I was moving it to this place—destroyed
—have been loaded with execrations, had all manner of evil
spoken of me falsely, and finally had my life threatened, and
laid down at night, weary and sick, with the expectation that I
might be aroused by the stealthy step of the assassin. . . . Yet
none of these things move me from my purpose; by the grace
of God I will not, I will not forsake my principles; and I will
maintain, and propagate them with all the means He puts into
my hands."[8]

On September 8, 1836, the new press for which his friends
had immediately subscribed arrived at Alton and Lovejoy
brought out the first issue of the Alton *Observer*. For several
months no one disturbed him or his work. Then in July, 1837,
Lovejoy, who was currently distributing petitions for the
American Anti-Slavery Society's campaign for congressional action against slavery, published a suggestion for the organization of an Illinois antislavery society. Worried citizens met
in the public market-house and solemnly listed their reasons
for opposing the editorial course of the *Observer*. They asked
the editor to cease publication of incendiary doctrines and the
chairman appointed a committee to inform him of the action.
In a written reply to the group Lovejoy declared that he hoped
"to discuss the overwhelmingly important subject of Slavery,
with the freedom of a republican and the meekness of a Christian."[9] He then referred the objectors to a recent *Observer* editorial in which he had reaffirmed the abolitionists' belief that

all men are born free and that masters should voluntarily give up their slaves. Those who disagreed with his views, he concluded, might use the columns of the *Observer* to refute them.

After this clash with the antiabolitionists, Elijah Lovejoy faced increasing opposition. He frequently heard threats against him and the *Observer* office. Then on August 21, 1837, angry men waylaid him in the darkness outside the city limits. But when he promised nonresistance if one of them would deliver his parcel of medicine to his sick wife, the crowd released him. God, he rejoiced later, had protected him. At about the same hour, however, another mob attacked the *Observer* office and completely destroyed the press.

So Elijah Lovejoy faced another crisis. Those who had been *Observer* supporters divided over the editor's policy. One group assisted him with plans for re-establishing the paper and responded so heartily to his appeal for funds that he was able to order a new press at once. The other group demanded that he keep the slavery question out of the paper and confine its columns strictly to religious matters. Lovejoy pondered the increasing difficulty of publishing his paper in Alton. Depression stalked the country and men who ordinarily supported causes had little money for philanthropy. The editor owed household debts and the *Observer* was on the verge of bankruptcy. In desperation Lovejoy made a last appeal to his friends.

On September 11 he addressed an open letter to the "Friends of the Redeemer in Alton." "Be it yours, brethren," he said, "to decide what is best for the cause of truth, most for the glory of God, and the salvation of souls, and rest assured—whatever my own private judgment may be—of my cordial acquiescence in your decision.

"I had, at first, intended to make an *unconditional* surrender of the editorship into your hands. But as such a course might be liable to misconstructions, I have, by the advice of a beloved brother, determined to leave the whole matter with you. I am ready to go forward if you say so, and equally ready to yield to a successor, if such be your opinion."

The only condition of his removal was "that you will assume in its behalf, all my obligations contracted in consequence of my connection with the 'Observer.' Some of them were contracted immediately on behalf of the 'Observer,' and some in supporting my family while its Editor.

"As I have now spent four among the best years of my life in struggling to establish the 'Observer,' and place it on its present footing, I shall expect you will furnish me with a sum sufficient to enable me to remove myself and family to another field of labour. . . .

"On these conditions I surrender into your hands the 'Observer's' subscription list. . . .

"May the spirit of wisdom, dear brethren, guide you to a wise and *unanimous* decision—to a decision which God will approve and ratify, and which shall redound to the glory of his name."[10]

As a committee of citizens met and decided to maintain the *Observer* in Alton but said nothing about retaining the editor, Lovejoy left for church meetings in St. Charles, Missouri. He and his wife and young son stayed in his mother-in-law's home. There St. Charles antiabolitionists found him. Twice in one night they entered and tried to drag him away. A third time rioters milled about the yard. Toward midnight Lovejoy slipped out and made his way in darkness to a friend's house on the road back to Alton. When he arrived home the following day he faced the destruction of his third press. On September 21 a mob had demolished it upon arrival. Although he knew not where he would re-establish himself, Lovejoy calmly ordered another press and continued preparation for an Illinois antislavery society.

While he waited for the new press Lovejoy joined with other abolitionists in a call to all those who "earnestly longed, and prayed for the immediate abolition of Slavery" to meet in Alton on October 26. Simultaneously, Edward Beecher, active antislavery man of the faculty of Illinois College at Jacksonville, issued a more inclusive invitation to the "friends of free discussion."[11] As a result of the conflicting wording, a fiery meeting ensued. Abolitionists answered the *Observer* notice and came to organize a state antislavery society. Antiabolitionists, led by state's attorney Usher F. Linder, declared that Beecher's note called them and they came to consider the dangers of such free discussion as Lovejoy's policies represented. In a brief but tense and boisterous session, the latter group overrode the antislavery men and pushed through resolutions which upheld the constitutional sanctions of slaveholding and then summarily adjourned the meeting. Dismayed but undaunted, the abolitionists next day met at a private home in Upper Alton and organized the Illinois Anti-Slavery Society. There they voted to re-establish the *Observer* with Lovejoy as editor and at the same time elected him secretary of the new organization.

The antislavery conflict in Alton now raced to a climax. Edward Beecher followed adjournment of the state meeting with a series of lectures in the Presbyterian church in Lower Alton. His friends, fearing trouble even though no mob appeared for the first talk, formed a "militia" company, supplied themselves with arms, and sent an emissary to ask the mayor to attend the second sermon in the knowledge that armed men were ready to obey his commands for keeping order in the town. At this lecture the guards sat tensely in the balcony. Beecher talked to an attentive audience. As he got well into his remarks a stone suddenly sailed through a window. Instantly a voice ordered, "To arms!" and the armed men jumped to attention. Shouldering their guns, Lovejoy's friends marched out to stand during the remainder of the talk with guns poised to protect the audience should the need arise. As Beecher concluded, the crowd filed out and found Mayor John Krum hustling all home, defenders as well as the boisterous young men who stood by and called the guards "cowards."[12]

During the next few days worried citizens met to discuss means of quieting the opposing factions in Alton. Edward Beecher stayed on to champion Lovejoy and the *Observer*; Usher F. Linder flayed the dangers of abolitionist doctrine.

The committee appointed to recommend a solution met and reported in favor of moderation and free discussion but suggested that the situation could best be resolved by Lovejoy's severing connection with any paper in Alton. All eyes turned to the *Observer* editor.

Deliberately Elijah Parish Lovejoy walked to the front of the committee room. He paused a long moment, then began slowly, "Mr Chairman—it is not true, as has been charged upon me, that I hold in contempt the feelings and sentiments of this community, in reference to the question which is now agitating it. . . . I have asked for nothing but to be protected in my rights as a citizen—rights which God has given me, and which are guaranteed to me by the constitution of my country. . . . But if I have been guilty of no violation of law, why am I hunted up and down continually like a partridge upon the mountains? Why am I threatened with the *tar-barrel?* Why am I waylaid every day, and from night to night, and my life in jeopardy every hour? . . . I know, sir, that you can tar and feather me, hang me up, or put me into the Mississippi, without the least difficulty. . . . I have been made to feel that if I am not safe at Alton, I shall not be safe any where. . . . And now if I leave here and go elsewhere, violence may overtake me in my retreat, and I have no more claim upon the protection of any other community than I have upon this; and I have concluded, after consultation with my friends, and earnestly seeking counsel of God, to *remain at Alton,* and here to insist on protection in the exercise of my rights. If the civil authorities refuse to protect me, I must look to God; and if I die, I have determined to make my grave in Alton."[13] In the spirit of the early Christians Lovejoy would welcome martyrdom. He returned to his journalism and awaited the arrival of a new press.

After the Beecher episode Lovejoy's friends of the militia company repeatedly called upon Mayor Krum and insisted that he accept command of their group. On every occasion the mayor gave the same reply. He could recognize only such military organizations as complied with the state law. He instructed them concerning that law. In early November, while Lovejoy daily expected delivery of his press, some fifty men answered a public call to organize a volunteer company "to act under direction of the Mayor, in defense of the law."[14] Some who came had heard nothing of any specific object for the organization; others thought they were to protect the incoming press, but believed this a separate activity from that of the militia unit.

At any rate, on November 6, 1837, men enrolled, paraded, and drilled with loaded guns in the warehouse of which William S. Gilman was part owner. This was the same building to which Lovejoy's press was shortly delivered. In the evening Gilman asked the armed men to volunteer to guard the building during the night. Some thirty agreed to stay. When the press arrived Mayor Krum responded to a call to supervise the peaceful landing and the defenders spent a quiet night in the warehouse. Meanwhile, Elijah Lovejoy was at home hoping to protect his family from a threatened mob.

On November 7, 1837, Gilman, worried about the armed guards in his warehouse, called upon the mayor and again asked that he take command of the "militia company." But the mayor would only approve the legality of such protection and promise that if an emergency did arise he would call upon the men there. Moreover, he insisted that he be the judge of whether or not an emergency existed at any given time. Gilman returned to the warehouse and prepared to retain the little group until the press could be moved. But events in Alton were moving faster than he knew.

On the night of November 7 Elijah Lovejoy and eighteen others settled down beside their guns in Gilman's warehouse. Until ten o'clock the town was quiet. At that hour two men came from the outside with a message that unless Gilman would surrender the press a fast-growing mob would demolish the building at once. Within a few minutes after Gilman's refusal, a shower of stones crashed against the building and the owner went to a second-story door to order the molesters away. Someone on the ground pointed a pistol directly in his face and

Gilman scampered back into the warehouse. As the mob finished splintering the glass from the last of the windows at one end of the building, shots sounded. From within came answering gunfire and a mobster toppled to the ground. For a time there was quiet.

The infuriated rioters carried their fallen colleague away to die. Soon they returned. This time they kept to a windowless side of the building and prepared to fire the structure. The mayor begged the defenders to release the press in order to forestall even more tragic events than those they had already witnessed. They would defend the press with their lives, said the guardsmen. A man clambered to the corner of the warehouse and succeeded in setting fire to the roof; the defenders dashed out and drove him away but could do nothing about the slowly burning flame on the roof. At that, most of the mobsters backed away from the building. Those inside believed that the rioters had retired.

But this night was to be memorable in the history of the antislavery crusade. Elijah Lovejoy and two other men stepped to the high door of the warehouse and stood looking about, their eyes surveying the damage and following the retreating mobites. But not all had gone. Suddenly a shot rang out and Lovejoy staggered backward. He clutched his chest and groped his way into the warehouse. As he tried to get up the little flight of stairs to the others, he fell for the last time, gasping, "Oh, God, I am shot. I am shot." For a while those inside were too stunned to move, but after a few minutes they hastily conferred with Gilman on the advisability of giving up the press to save other goods in the building. All agreed to surrender and shortly they sent word to the rioters still near the building that Lovejoy was dead. They asked that they be permitted to leave the warehouse unmolested. The attackers agreed. Quickly the press defenders secreted their guns and filed out as their enemies filed in. In quiet determination Lovejoy's opponents then destroyed the press and retired to their homes.[15]

Abolition had its first martyr and abolitionists everywhere

hailed the fallen Elijah. The *Liberator* appeared draped in heavy black lines with screaming banners. "HORRID TRAGEDY," it shouted, and chronicled the complete story, including a statement from Mayor Krum on the doings of the entire tragic week in Alton. The *Salem Gazette* cried, " 'The blood of the martyrs is the seed of the church.' The murder of Lovejoy, by the servile and bloody panders of Slavery, in Illinois, A FREE STATE, will do more to drive a nail into the coffin of 'the Patriarchal System' than a living Lovejoy could effect in a century of effort."[16] Garrison, who disapproved Lovejoy's resort to arms to protect his property, nevertheless exclaimed, "The amiable, benevolent, intrepid LOVEJOY is no more!"

"Thanks be to God," he continued editorially, "though being dead, he yet speaks!—for his spirit lives, and is walking abroad over the land, terrifying a guilty, conscience-stricken people by its presence; and from his grave is heard a cry of blood, in tones that pierce the heavens and shake the earth. . . . In his martyrdom he died as the representative of Philanthropy, Justice, Liberty, and Christianity. . . ." The *New Yorker* called him a martyr to public liberty. The *Emancipator* declared that November 7 would henceforth be a marked day on the calendar and suggested the epitaph:

A MARTYR
TO THE FURY OF A FREE PEOPLE
MURDERING
IN DEFENCE OF SLAVERY

The Lynn *Record* called Lovejoy a martyr whose memory every patriot and philanthropist should embalm in his breast. The *Herald of Freedom* said, "The blood of martyrdom has begun to flow. . . . The first sacrifice to the god of American Oppression has been offered." Other papers proclaimed him a martyr to freedom of the press, to civil liberty. The *Liberator* announced that when Lovejoy's mother heard of his death she said, " 'Tis well! I would rather my son had fallen a martyr to his cause, than that he proved recreant to his principles.' "[17]

Said the *Republican and Eagle* of Homer, New York, "In any way in which this matter can be viewed, Mr. Lovejoy was a martyr to the cause of American Liberty, the cause of the Constitution, the rights of man and the laws of Heaven. . . . He fell in defence of his castle, his property, his family, his country, and humanity." To the *Massachusetts Spy* he had "fallen a martyr to the sacred right of Americans, to think for themselves, and to speak what they think." What must be the condition of society, asked the New York *Observer,* when conduct such as Lovejoy's endangers a man's life? Under a row of hands with index fingers pointing to the article, the Gettysburg *Star and Republican Banner* proclaimed Lovejoy a victim of the lawless spirit of slavery. Dozens of poems to the honor of his martyrdom filled the poetry sections of as many papers. Down in Kentucky, however, the editor of the Louisville *Herald* foretold the chief result of Lovejoy's death. Every drop of blood the martyred Elijah shed, he declared, would sow a new abolition society.[18]

Ministers of every denomination preached Lovejoy sermons. Many thought of him as the St. Stephen of his time. In a sermon which he delivered in Dover, New Hampshire, the Reverend David Root took as his text, "And devout men carried Stephen to his burial and made great lamentation over him." Stephen, he said, fell a victim of a mob called out by clerical hypocrites whom Lovejoy's enemies resembled. Stephen's death did not stop the spread of Christianity and so it would be with Lovejoy and abolition. ". . . for out of his ashes," said Root, "shall arise a noble company of martyrs. . . . I invoke the 'ministers of the Gospel' in our land, without distinction of denomination, to bring the dead body of the Alton martyr to their meeting houses, all gory in its blood, and lay it down before all the people, that they may look upon it and be filled with indignation and horror. . . ."[19] In New York City and in Utica, Beriah Greene proclaimed that since the deaths of Stephen and Antipas the awful circumstance of sealing one's testimony to the truth with his blood, had entered into the definition of a martyr. Lovejoy died as a witness to truth, Lovejoy was a martyr. *"For the inalienable rights of man—for every man, therefore, for whom they are inalienable—Lovejoy bowed his head in death. . . . 'He laid down his life for us, and we ought to lay down our lives for the brethren,'"* Greene concluded. To the fallen Lovejoy he addressed the words, "For thee, brother, why should we mourn? Thou has found thy place by the side of Stephen, in the glorious army of martyrs who now exult in the smiles of the Captain of their salvation."[20] William Ellery Channing declared in a letter to the *Liberator* that Lovejoy had died for liberties which must be protected.[21]

Groups as well as individuals expressed themselves on Lovejoy's death. The Rhode Island Anti-Slavery Society, meeting in Providence on November 28, 1837, adopted resolutions which said, in part, that Lovejoy died a martyr to great principles and that our only safety lay in perseverance for the rights of all men.[22] The Board of Managers of the Massachusetts Anti-Slavery Society declared that "On the 7th of November, 1837, the abolition cause, which had passed through many an ordeal of violence, received a BAPTISM OF BLOOD."[23] His martyrdom, they said, accomplished in an hour what individual exertion otherwise could not have effected for liberty. In presenting the annual report of the anniversary meeting in May, 1838, the members of the Executive Committee of the American Anti-Slavery Society said they did so "with renewed confidence that the enterprise which has been committed to their care, enjoys the favor of Almighty God. The seal which He has always set upon every successful and glorious reformation, He has suffered to be estamped upon this. Our principles now speaking through the blood of the martyred LOVEJOY, partake visibly of that efficacy which eighteen centuries ago smote into dust the chains of idolatry. . . ."[24]

Citizens in various places met to commemorate Lovejoy's death. Residents of Lynn met on November 22 and a few days later the Boston Young Men's Anti-Slavery Society held a brief ceremony on Thanksgiving afternoon.[25] In their November 27 meeting Philadelphians agreed that Lovejoy had died defending his God-given right of free discussion. Without this right, they declared, other rights became valueless.[26] A fiery meeting was that of December 8, 1837, in Boston's Faneuil Hall. At first the mayor and council had refused the use of the building for such purpose, but when William E. Channing added his voice to the request, they agreed. Above the noisy objections of the crowd Wendell Phillips refuted Attorney-General James T. Austin's contention that the rioters at Alton constituted an "orderly mob" of patriots and that Elijah Lovejoy had "died as a fool dieth." Of the martyr Phillips said, "He took refuge under the banner of liberty,—amid its folds; and when he fell, its glorious stars and stripes, the emblem of free institutions, around which cluster so many heart-stirring memories, were blotted out in the martyr's blood."[27] On December 22 the Massachusetts Anti-Slavery Society met, and Amos A. Phelps reviewed Lovejoy's life and blamed the Catholics for most of his troubles. Orestes Brownson followed and declared him a martyr to free speech. High point of the session was Garrison's outright support of Lovejoy for the first time. Oh, how he wished, he said, that they could bring in Lovejoy's dead body, followed by a train of manacled and sorrow-stricken slaves supporting the living, insensible, agonized wife! A meeting in Portland, Maine, resolved that God had permitted Lovejoy to fall a martyr to human rights. Individuals and societies collected money for the destitute family.[28]

Lovejoy's martyrdom was at once the rallying cry for abolitionists. The martyr's brothers quickly wrote a memoir of him and published it within a year after his death. In 1839 the state antislavery society in Maine appropriated money to publish a copy of his life story for each state and one for the Library of Congress.[29] His death became a symbol of the steadfastness of abolitionists. On April 5, 1860, Elijah's brother Owen, member of the House of Representatives from an Illinois district, told his colleagues as they discussed the extension of slavery, "You may kill Cassius M. Clay, as you threaten to do; but 'the blood

Above: Again and again mobs destroyed Elijah Lovejoy's presses because he printed abolitionist literature. This picture shows the burning of the building which housed one of his presses after the press itself has been thrown into the Mississippi. *Below:* Here an angry mob smashes Lovejoy's press. "A Printing Press Demolished at Slavery's Bidding" is the caption of this picture from *The American Anti-Slavery Almanac* of 1839.

Above: George Storrs dragged from the pulpit in Northfield, N.H. as he prays for the freeing of the slaves. A picture from *The American Anti-Slavery Almanac* entitled "A Minister Arrested for Preaching Against Sin." *Below:* Expulsion of abolitionists from Tremont Temple, Boston. A drawing from *Harper's Weekly* of December 15, 1860 which illustrates the typical reaction to abolitionist propaganda.

of the martyrs is the seed of the church.' You may shed his blood, as you shed the blood of my brother on the banks of the Mississippi twenty years ago—and what then? I am here today, thank God, to vindicate the principles baptized in his blood."[30] In 1881 a book reviewer who reviewed the recently published *The Martyrdom of Lovejoy,* by Henry Tanner of Alton, a press defender with Lovejoy in 1837, declared: "No personal incident of the antislavery struggle—the fate of John Brown excepted— made so profound an impression on the North as the murder of Lovejoy."[31] In a speech in 1888 in the Church of the Unity in St. Louis, Thomas Dimmock found his audience much interested in his story of the reburial of the Alton martyr.[32] As late as 1898, Samuel D. Hastings of Wisconsin wrote a New York paper, "With the exception of John Brown's raid and his subsequent hanging by the state of Virginia, the murder of Lovejoy exerted a greater influence in arousing the people of the nation as to the true character of the institution of slavery and in hastening the day of its downfall than any other one event."[33] On November 8, 1897, the Lovejoy Monument Association dedicated in Alton a monument to the martyr's memory for which the state legislature of Illinois bore some five-sixths of the cost. In 1930 posterity put its final mark of approval upon the life and martyrdom of Elijah P. Lovejoy when the Illinois Press Association made him the first editor to be honored in the Editors' Hall of Fame at the state university.[34]

Before the year 1837 many an abolitionist had suffered for conscience's sake; all had welcomed persecution for its advantage to the cause of the slave. After Lovejoy's death the call to martyrdom rang loud in the ear of every spokesman for the Negro's freedom. Their endurance of maltreatment rapidly became the very fiber of antislavery lore.

With
Steady
Step

FOR a decade after Lovejoy, lust for martyrdom permeated abolition ranks. Man after man gloried in his suffering for the cause. Their sacrifices, real and imaginary, fleshened out the martyr story. The Civil War generation could look back upon a long line of sufferers for the Negro's freedom, for abolition martyrs both preceded and followed Elijah Lovejoy. Prudence Crandall, Theodore Weld, James G. Birney and a host of less eminent men contributed each his bit to perpetuating and emphasizing the martyr tradition.

Even before Lovejoy's death, in a little New England town, a heroic woman made a bid for the martyr's crown. Prudence Crandall tried to save Negroes from the depths of ignorance into which the master class would keep them. Everyone believed in education and believed that through education nations might be made great, but the boon of education was to be denied the daughters of Africa.

In the fall of 1832 Quakeress Prudence Crandall opened a school in Canterbury, Windham County, Connecticut and invited the young women of the community to enroll. As she prepared to start her classes one Sarah Harris, a seventeen year old Negress whose father farmed nearby, applied for admission. Miss Crandall knew that the girl had attended the district school and learned that she had an exemplary record there for both scholarship and deportment. She admitted Sarah Harris as a pupil and the other girls accepted her just as they had in the public school.

Shortly, however, some parents began to complain that they had not expected that in a private school their daughters would attend classes with a "nigger." Indeed, they said, their children must not receive instruction beside any member of the inferior Negro race. They could, of course, Miss Crandall told them, withdraw their children. Immediately many parents did just that.

But for all her courageous stand, Prudence Crandall then faced a financial as well as a socio-political problem. She had purchased the home which housed the school and to avoid loss of her entire investment she would have to continue the project. For days she pondered a solution. Then she hit upon a new plan. Since the whites had chosen to leave her school, she would conduct classes exclusively for colored girls. Hastily she sent advertisements to abolition journals and appealed to Negro residents of Philadelphia, Boston, and other Northern cities.

When Canterbury residents learned of Prudence Crandall's decision they were furious. The town leaders called an indignation meeting. But the teacher hoped to overcome their objections. In Samuel J. May, minister and antislavery lecturer, George W. Benson, active abolitionist relative of William Lloyd Garrison, and Arnold Buffum, lecturing agent for the New England Anti-Slavery Society, she had the assistance of three men experienced in the excesses of antiabolitionism. Had they been permitted to speak at the meeting, the troubles might have been resolved in short order, for Miss Crandall was ready to compromise. She was willing to move her school to a less conspicuous part of town if the objectors would help her dispose of her house without financial loss. But spokesmen for the indignant townspeople brushed aside her advisers as one Andrew T. Judson, near whose fine home the school stood, overrode the regularly appointed moderator, ranted against permitting out-of-state colored people to enter private schools in Connecticut, and peremptorily demanded that the meeting adjourn. Although Samuel May jumped to his feet and coaxed most of those attending to remain to hear Miss Crandall's story, he could do little except answer Judson's remarks before his audience drifted away. Judson had destroyed the chance for amicable settlement.

Prudence Crandall concluded that she had no choice but to proceed with her decision to conduct a school for Negroes. Hence some fifteen or twenty colored girls shortly arrived from several Northern cities and classes began. But Canterbury residents rose to battle. Some urged the civil authorities to revive an old vagrant law which would force nonresidents to depart within a stated time or pay a fine for every week they remained after warning, with whipping the extreme penalty for disobeying the law. Several town leaders pressed for enforcement of this law despite the fact that Samuel May had given bond that the students would not become a burden upon the community. Tension gripped the town.

Meanwhile, the ubiquitous Andrew T. Judson had been seeing members of the state legislature. As a result, on May 24, 1833, that body passed a law prohibiting the establishment of schools for out-of-state students unless the schoolmaster had the written consent of the civil authorities in the affected town and of the selectmen thereof. Canterbury greeted the news of the law with the ringing of church bells and much hand-shaking.

Prudence Crandall had not long to wait to be caught by the new law. On June 27 officers came to the school and took her away for immediate arraignment. Her trial would come up for the next session of the superior court at Brooklyn in August. In the intervening time she could raise several hundred dollars bail or she could go to jail. Numerous antislavery friends would gladly go her bond. But Samuel May thought the martyrdom of a brief imprisonment would do a great good for the cause of antislavery. Miss Crandall agreed, and May went quietly around to her friends with instructions that they were not to give bond for her.

So Prudence Crandall went to jail. Publicly May announced that the authorities would thrust upon the young woman the added disgrace of incarceration in a room occupied until recently by a convicted murderer. Indeed, May insisted that she have that particular cell, on the contention that it was the most comfortable in the building. Without publicity, he supervised its cleaning, arranged for someone to stay with her, and had a bed moved from his own home for her. The preparations completed, Prudence Crandall spent one night in jail at Brooklyn, Connecticut, for the good of the abolition cause. The next day her friends bailed her out. Abolition journals diligently recounted her sufferings.

The Crandall difficulties, however, had scarcely begun; so also had the effectiveness of her persecution. On August 23, 1833, she appeared for trial in Brooklyn County Court, Judge Joseph Eaton presiding. Her indictment rested upon two counts, scarcely separable: contrary to the new law she had accepted nonresident colored pupils and she had instructed these pupils. Andrew T. Judson thundered for the prosecution and explained at length that the district schools provided education for Connecticut Negro children and that anyone who brought others into the state threatened the people with additional tax burdens. The jury listened, went out, came back for additional instruction, went out again, and finally gave up to receive discharge as a hung jury.

Prudence Crandall and her friends waited impatiently through more weeks of delay. Then her case came up again and a jury declared her guilty of violating the new state law. But in July, 1834, the Connecticut Supreme Court reversed the decision of the lower court and ended her legal difficulties.

Meanwhile, residents of Canterbury continued their persecution. In the summer of 1834 rowdies attempted to burn down her house. Abolitionists reported that no citizen would sell or give her food, no physician would wait upon her or her pupils, a mob smeared her house with filth and polluted the well beyond any hope of cleaning or restoring it. On September 9 rioters attacked her home, destroying window sashes and demolishing some ninety window panes. Much as she wished to continue the fight, Prudence Crandall finally recognized that she could not withstand such opposition. In late 1834 she closed her school.

Although she lost her personal antislavery struggle, Prudence Crandall contributed to the martyr legend the proof that Negro girls might not learn in the company of their white sisters. Her story constituted a valuable chapter in abolition lore, and shortly the state antislavery society found the sale of her portrait an effective source of revenue.

While Prudence Crandall was struggling to enrich the Negro's life with the beauties of literature, thus securing to herself a niche in abolition's roster, and while Lovejoy was penning indignant editorials, Theodore Dwight Weld, organizer and agitator, was winning for himself the title "Most mobbed man in America." Weld was among those abolition workers whose persecutions became legend. A large man with a great head of bushy hair and solemn, deep-set eyes, he had a commanding voice which stung both friends and foes to action. Of him a writer in the *Pittsburg Times* said in 1834: "Mr. Weld is one of Nature's orators—not a declaimer, but a logician of great tact and power. His inexhaustible fund of anecdote and general information, with the power of being intensely pathetic, enables him to give the greatest imaginable interest to the subject. His powers of teaching are of the first order—that is, his facility for generalizing broadly and regularly, for passing into profound abstractions and bringing his wealth of ideas into beautiful light by clear, striking, and familiar illustrations."[1] During the time in which Weld preached the cause through the Ohio valley, the Western Reserve, and western New York, he became at one and the same time the most successful of abolitionizers and the most mobbed man in the field.

Born in 1803, Weld was the son of a western New York preacher-farmer. He owed the vigor of his religious zeal to the master evangelist Charles Grandison Finney and owed his anti-slavery fervor to Charles Stuart, Jamaica-born exponent of British emancipation. In 1825 Finney converted Weld and accepted him for his "Holy Band" of assistants. After two years of the work, Weld determined to enter the ministry and in 1827, with a number of Finney converts, entered Oneida Institute at Whitesborough, New York. There Charles Stuart paid his expenses and through letters, pamphlets, and tracts constantly begged him to turn his great talent to the abolition cause. Indeed, the reform field was not new to Weld. As a very young man he had toured the South and West, giving lectures on the art of memory; he had served as agent for the Oneida Institute; he had spent school vacations lecturing in the West for the American Temperance Society. After several years, Stuart's efforts were successful; in 1834 Weld mounted the abolition rostrum.

In January, 1834, Weld began his lecture tour for the American Anti-Slavery Society with specific commission to Ohio and possible assignment by the Executive Committee to additional areas. Weld brought the techniques of the Finney revival to the abolition crusade. Preaching the sin of slavery, he followed the plan of the protracted meeting. His lectures lasted from two to five hours and a series continued for from five to twenty consecutive nights, depending upon how long it took to convert his audiences to abolitionism. In the manner of the great Finney, Weld, at the close of each series, called upon his "converts" to rise to acknowledge conversion. Hence in dozens of communities he left a little nucleus of believers to form abolition societies and to carry on the holy work.

In 1834, however, abolitionism frightened many Americans. William Lloyd Garrison's insistence upon immediatism was not only dividing active abolitionists over the question of how and when to free the slaves; it was also leading to charges that abolitionists would flood the North with free Negroes, that they encouraged intermarriage, in short that abolitionism was a threat to the Constitution and the American Way of that day. Hence abolition lecturers might expect any kind of reception from American audiences. Theodore Dwight Weld experienced all kinds.

In 1835, in Oldtown, Ohio, Weld's hearers threatened violence to his person. Yet he won them over in five lectures and left a sizeable group pledged to continue his work. At Granville residents peremptorily drove him out of town. In Circleville he obtained the use of the Episcopal vestry only after great difficulty. Then at his second lecture a mob gathered to throw stones and then rotten eggs through the windows. When a rock hit him squarely in the forehead, Weld staggered, paused only until dizziness ceased, then completed his lecture. On the next day, while his head still throbbed painfully, a mob again congregated and threatened further injury. The church trustees feared for their property. Quickly they found him a lecture room in a store building as far removed from the church as possible. The rioters followed to disturb his first lecture there with the crashing of stones and clubs against the shutters. When they were unable to frighten him, they gathered outside to curse and to brandish lampblack, large nails, stones, and rotten eggs, all the while shouting how they would make use of each for him. They persisted for several nights and Weld permitted a small guard of friends to escort him to his lodgings after each lecture. But at the end of the week, Circleville quieted down and formed a new antislavery society.

In the fall of 1835 Weld gave a series of lectures in Chardon. At his first appearance one man arose and demanded time to read to the assembly resolutions adopted the previous August by a Boston antiabolitionist meeting. Weld asked that he wait until the end of the lecture. Loud voices called for the resolutions and the stranger shouted his way through the entire list. When the audience quieted, Weld went on. Then rioters serenaded with tin horns, sleigh bells, and drums and pelted the women with rotten eggs as the audience departed.

At Painesville, Weld's next stop, mobites stoned him on his

first day in town. The second day a citizens' meeting, with the mayor as chairman, adopted antiabolitionist resolutions and included one which directed Weld to leave town. He calmly gave the notification committee a convincing "No" and continued the series. The Common Council asked him to go away. Again he refused. When, at the fifth lecture, a prominent citizen, militia general J. H. Payne, led in a noisy group, charged the lecturer with treason and violation of the Constitution, and dared him to give one more lecture, Weld took the dare and lectured next day. When he left Painesville one hundred people had already enrolled in the new antislavery society. Later a mob in Putnam, Ohio, smashed the windows and doors of the hall in which he spoke. They tore the gate from the enclosing fence; they waylaid Weld after the session and gave him a beating; they attacked colored people for daring to attend.

In June, 1836, Weld almost achieved a complete martyrdom. At that time he entered Troy, New York, to win the town for his cause. But Troy was obstinate. At the first big meeting groups of angry listeners several times rushed down the aisle to drag him from the pulpit. Courageous friends and his own fearless stance saved him. Some pitched stones, pieces of brick, eggs, coins, and sticks at him as he spoke. He dodged the close ones and thundered away against American slavery. Some of the men followed him to his lodgings, and, despite his friends' protective escort, he suffered more than one severe beating. In the end, the mob won, for Weld had spent his voice and strength and, for once, he left a town with little gain for abolition. With his voice and physical stamina permanently impaired, Weld left the lecture field.

Later in 1836 Weld helped select and train the seventy antislavery lecturers which the American Anti-Slavery Society shortly sent out. The next year he took a desk at the organization's New York headquarters. There he supervised the placement of lecturing agents and edited special publications. He published his Bible argument against slavery under the title *Is Slavery from Above or Beneath,* condensed and partially rewrote a study made by two others of the results of emancipation in Antigua, Barbados, and Jamaica, and gathered a number of his newspaper articles for publication as *The Power of Congress over the District of Columbia*. Later, with the help of his wife, Angelina Grimké Weld, whom he married in 1838, he revised his Bible argument as the *Bible Against Slavery*. For three years he edited the national society's annual almanacs. Asked by that group's Executive Committee to present to Americans a true picture of chattel slavery, he prepared, this time aided by Angelina and her sister, Sarah, *American Slavery As It Is: Testimony of a Thousand Witnesses*. In 1841 and 1842 he worked in Washington as research expert and antislavery adviser to John Quincy Adams and his small group of champions of the right of petition. He returned to his New York farm in late winter of the latter year. Thereafter Weld left active antislavery agitation to others, many of whom he had first fired with abolition zeal.

Theodore Weld was a martyr in the spirit of the early Christians. To a fellow lecturer in the cause he wrote of the Troy affair, "Let every abolitionist debate the matter once for all, and settle it with himself whether he is an abolitionist from *impulse* or *principle*—whether he can lie upon the rack—and clasp the faggot and tread with steady step the scaffold—whether he can stand at the post of duty and having done all and suffered all, stand—and if cloven down, fall and die a martyr 'not accepting deliverance.' "[2] Theodore Weld was himself the embodiment of the martyr who stood at his post to do all and to suffer all for the poor slave.

While Weld was making a career of abolition, James G. Birney made tremendous sacrifices of wealth and a comfortable home for the abolition crusade. Forsaking all—even as Jesus had said to the rich young man, "If thou wilt be perfect, go and sell that thou hast, and give to the poor, and thou shalt have treasure in heaven: and come and follow me"—Birney took up the fight for the Negro's freedom.

Born in Danville, Kentucky, in 1792, Birney enjoyed an excellent education and in 1810 returned home to accept the responsibilities and pleasures of his family's wealth and prestige. Almost at once he took his place with Kentucky's leaders. At the age of twenty-four he was a member of the state legislature working to keep that body from effecting an arrangement whereby Kentucky would join with Ohio and Indiana in strengthening the fugitive slave laws. Simultaneously, he urged some kind of gradual emancipation law for the state.

In 1818 Birney removed to Alabama and entered politics there, beginning immediately to campaign for a state constitution favorable to gradual emancipation. When his efforts were unsuccessful, he asked the state legislature to consider a bill providing jury trial for slaves indicted for crimes above petty larceny. Seven years later when he was no longer in the legislature but was an agent for the American Colonization Society, his influence was the greatest single force behind the passage of a law forbidding the importation of slaves into the state either for sale or for hire. When after two years he gave up the Colonization Society agency and returned to residence in Kentucky, he worked hard in an unsuccessful attempt to get that state, as well as Virginia and Tennessee, to abolish the slave trade.

In 1832 Birney and Weld met at the home of a mutual friend. Weld talked antislavery and Birney listened. When Weld left to continue his lecture tour, Birney renounced colonization for abolition and two years later freed his own slaves. In 1835, as vice-president of the American Anti-Slavery Society, he traveled through Northern states urging state legislators to support emancipation plans. That year he delivered the principal address at the annual meeting of the society in New York.

Also in 1835, Birney issued a prospectus for an antislavery paper which he intended to establish in his native Danville. The townspeople displayed such hostility, however, that he moved to Cincinnati. But he was no better off there, for irate citizens distributed inflammatory handbills which offered rewards for his head, and mobs looted his office three times. Angry men threatened to kill him and on one occasion might have done so had Birney not been able to talk to them so convincingly. Indeed, Birney knew whereof he spoke when in 1842 he wrote abolitionist friends, "Our adversaries are numerous and powerful; but let us remember that in this struggle they are also the adversaries of Justice, of Mercy, of Humanity, of Religion, of God; against whom they cannot prevail."

In 1837 Birney went to New York as secretary for the American Anti-Slavery Society. Until May, 1840, he attended local antislavery conventions and visited state legislatures. He spoke against the extension of slavery, against anti-Negro laws, and for the enactment of personal-liberty laws and the privilege of jury trial for Negroes charged with breaking the laws which protected slavery. His work held the national organization together and the number of auxiliary societies increased rapidly. Under his supervision the national society in one year published 725,000 copies of its tracts and pamphlets.

Between Birney and Garrison, however, there was little kinship of spirit. Birney could not abide the techniques which Garrison used. Where the former was moderate, the latter was rash. Birney's calm, logical statements contrasted sharply with Garrison's fiery, vituperative ones. After Birney assumed leadership in the national antislavery society his followers were in constant conflict with the Garrisonites over the question of whether the abolition of slavery was a moral or a political problem. While the Garrison faction proclaimed that the Constitution's acceptance of the sinful institution made legal abolition an impossibility under that document, the Birneyites prepared to disprove their contention. In 1839 the Birney group followed their leader into the new Liberty Party in the hope of electing to office men who would legislate slavery out of existence. The Garrisonites withdrew from the Birney-sympathizing American Anti-Slavery Society and after 1840 continued their moral crusade against slavery through a new organization, the American and Foreign Anti-Slavery Society. In that year Birney became the new party's unsuccessful presidential candidate. Shortly thereafter a riding accident limited his activity to the writing of tracts and pamphlets for political abolitionism.

James G. Birney could have had honor, prestige, and wealth in either Kentucky or Alabama, the two states where he had already established homes. But he heeded Jesus' advice to the rich young man and forsook his wealth and the easy life to become an unhonored zealot of the antislavery crusade.

By 1840 Prudence Crandall, Theodore Weld, and James G. Birney had demonstrated in life as Elijah Lovejoy had demonstrated in death, traits which Americans could recognize as worthy of Christian martyrs. Miss Crandall's adversaries had driven her from the field, but only after she had proved that Northerners would not tolerate the education of black children in the same classes with white. Defeated, she yet wore her martyr's crown in dignity. Theodore Weld established the truth that the genuine abolitionist stood in the face of all persecution, ready to die for the Negro's freedom. Sacrificing both bodily strength and the power of his magnificent voice, he was both martyr to the cause and glorious inspiration to fellow laborers in the holy crusade against slavery in America. James G. Birney demonstrated the zealot's readiness to forego wealth, prestige, and the pleasures of a comfortable home and an indulgent family to battle for emancipation. In his renunciation of the advantages which he might have enjoyed he was a living example of Jesus' assertion that heaven may be earned not by love of earth's goods but by love of earth's unfortunate humans. In Birney, the rich young man for whom the martyr's crown glowed brighter than did his golden wealth, Americans saw a martyr to conscience. Meanwhile, other abolitionists continued the crusade in the martyr tradition.

Weep Not For Me

WHILE Prudence Crandall, Theodore Weld, Elijah Lovejoy, and James G. Birney made each a contribution to the martyr tradition in antislavery lore, other abolition crusaders followed in the footsteps of those men of Biblical days who suffered imprisonment or physical torture for their beliefs. In the early 1840's these men added their stories to abolition records.

Even as Paul and Silas went to jail for preaching the Word of God, dozens of men who pleaded for the Negro's freedom landed behind bars. Among the many so punished were three jailed at Palmyra, Missouri, in 1841, nearly four years after the death of the martyred Lovejoy. Civil authorities in Palmyra accused Alanson Work, James E. Burr, and George Thompson of attempting to assist slaves across the Mississippi River to free soil. They dealt accordingly with them.

James Burr was a man of about forty who lived with his wife and four children at the Mission Institute at Quincy, Illinois.

Alanson Work and George Thompson were theological students there. Betrayed by the slaves they hoped to liberate and captured some distance from Palmyra, the men marched before the guns of Missouri officers on an overnight journey back to that place. There they spent two and a half months in jail while they awaited trial.

"We desired the liberation of the slaves," wrote Thompson later. "God knew how to bring it about, better than we did. We longed to be instrumental in doing something for our brethren in bonds. God granted us our hearts' desire. And a happy day for the slaves of Missouri was it, when we were taken captive, bound, and incarcerated in their midst. This was placing the light just where it was most needed—in the dense darkness— and where it made visible the abominations that prevailed. Blessed be God! . . . To die for the slave I felt willing, if this was the thing needed—the Lord being Judge. . . . We rejoice in our chains."[1]

"Pray that we may be Christlike," wrote Work to his wife.[2]

During the first ten weeks of incarceration the three men received visits from friends, and read Foxe's *Book of Martyrs* and other religious books which their visitors brought them. Thompson wrote of his prison experiences to the congregation of his home church, and the abolition journals published his every word and added the narrative of his preaching to the other inmates of the jail. The similarity of the men in the Missouri jail to the imprisoned martyrs of the early Christian church added an impressive chapter to the chronicle of American abolitionism.

"We all rejoiced in our sufferings—each sympathized with the other, our hearts beat in sweet unison, and all were willing to go to the Penitentiary, or *die*, if need be, for the deliverance of the oppressed," Thompson later declared.[3]

Indeed, the men needed their strong faith and enduring courage. On September 10, 1841, Burr, Work, and Thompson, followed by a grumbling mob, went under guard to the courthouse. They were, declared the state's attorney, as wicked as

Mormons and as lawless as land pirates. But, said their counsel, even though a Missouri law to judge their action larceny might exist—and this he doubted—a penitentiary sentence, even if they deserved it, as many people said, would only martyrize them and so encourage more abolitionism. But his contentions went unheeded. Three days later, while a mob prepared to hang them if the court proved lenient, the three received sentence of twelve years in the state penitentiary and became martyrs in the image of St. Paul.

"Does anyone ask how we feel in view of our sentence?" they asked in a letter widely circulated in abolition papers. "We answer, happy, contented, cheerful, willing that God shall take us, and make us just such instruments of advancing His cause, as he sees best; being assured that our King will cause 'the wrath of man to praise Him;' and extend the great cause of *Liberty* by our unworthy sufferings."[4]

Back in his chains in the Palmyra jail to await removal to prison, Thompson wrote to a friend: ". . . and if *I* am thus to be sacrificed, I submit cheerfully, rejoicing that I am counted worthy to suffer shame for the name of Jesus."[5]

For over three years abolitionists constantly reminded the public of their colleagues in prison in Missouri. "Ye who have wept for the persecutions of the godly in ancient ages, draw nigh, and behold what slavery hath done—what Henry Clay and compromise have wrought," wrote Alvan Stewart in the *Friend of Man.* "This very case of these martyred young men, should string every antislavery man's arm with fresh power and energy, to conquer the recklessness of proslavery opinions, and create that grand mass of living, acting, and conquering humanity, which shall strike every fetter from the slave, and overturn the Penitentiary walls of Missouri, and again make our brothers free men."[6]

Then on January 20, 1845, the governor of Missouri pardoned Alanson Work on condition that he return to his native Connecticut. Ten days later Burr went free, although his pardon carried no restricting conditions. Five months later Thompson received the same kind of dismissal.

During the long months in prison Burr, Work, and Thompson conducted themselves in the manner of the martyrs in whose steps they followed. They thanked God for the privilege of suffering for faith and rejoiced in their contribution to the deliverance of the Negro in bondage. "And at midnight Paul and Silas prayed, and sang praises unto God: and the prisoners heard them," said the Bible. Three men in a Missouri prison demonstrated that even as Paul and Silas and a host of others, abolitionists could honor the prisons which bound them.

But it was yet to be demonstrated that a man would endure extreme physical torture for love of the enslaved millions. Jesus had patiently borne his crown of thorns and passively endured the nails of crucifixion in his hands and his feet. In the crusade for the Negro's freedom it remained for a New England workman to emulate the submission of the Son of God who had suffered all for His Father's earthly children.

In 1844 Jonathan Walker, a shipwright of Norwich, Massachusetts, who had spent the winter working at his trade along the Gulf of Mexico, agreed to use a small vessel which he had purchased for salvage work, to transport several Negroes to the Bahamas. Within a few days after they left Pensacola, Walker became so ill from exposure and fatigue that he was unable to share his meager knowledge of seamanship with the frightened Negroes, and after several days of dangerous passage, a wrecker, out of Key West, took Walker and his exhausted passengers aboard and towed the little vessel to home port.

At Key West officers took Walker before a magistrate who accused him of aiding Negroes to escape and set his bail at one thousand dollars. Walker was to appear before the court in November. But since he had no bondsmen, he went to jail immediately, first in the constable's home and then in government barracks. On July 13 his captors chained his hands and feet, placed him in the filthy hold of a steamboat, and escorted him on a six-day journey to Pensacola Navy Yard. On July 19 a deputy marshal conducted him to the town. Arraigned there, the judge asked for ten thousand dollars bail. Unable to post so large an amount, Walker went to jail to await trial. There, restrained by an ankle shackle and log chain, without chair or table, Walker sat, ate, and slept on the floor. During the months of his imprisonment four young children from a nearby home screamed for hours each day beneath his window.

On November 14, 1844, Jonathan Walker stood trial in the federal court in Escambia County, in the district of West Florida. The jury considered four indictments against him and recommended three punishments. First, he spent an hour in the pillory that stood before the courthouse. Next the United States marshal officiated for the branding of the letters "SS," for slave stealer, just below the prisoner's right thumb. For the remainder of his punishment—a fine of $150 and court costs— Walker went back to jail. There he received notice that he faced three more writs for trespass and damage. He owed the owners of the slaves he had tried to help some $106,000. When he went before the magistrate to answer the new charges he needed another three thousand dollars bail. Walker went back to jail, this time again in irons. His second trial came up on May 9, 1845, and the jury found him guilty of kidnapping three slaves and fined him five dollars for each. In addition, he was to remain in custody until he could pay court costs and the total expense of his imprisonment. When Walker's abolitionist friends finally collected money to free him, they paid an itemized bill for the period of his incarceration.

Antislavery newspapers followed the case with weekly stories. Each reprinted those of others. John G. Whittier wrote the poem *The Branded Hand,* and the abolition journals published it with a detailed drawing of Walker's branded palm. After his release on June 16, 1845, Walker himself made the rounds of newspaper offices, displayed his brand, and announced that he would write a complete account of his experience with the justice of slaveholders. The *Emancipator and Chronicle* declared that he should show his hand all over the state, for the paper had received more orders for the issue with the hand picture than it could possibly fill. Other admirers praised him for naming his children for great abolitionists—William Wilberforce, Lydia Child, and William Lloyd Garrison; they collected money and gathered clothing for his family. Walker meetings convened all over Massachusetts. At each, antislavery men told the Walker story and emphasized the cruelty of the slaveholders. After his release and return home Walker himself made an extensive lecture tour, told his story, and displayed the branded hand.

"Daughters of Jerusalem, weep not for me, but weep for yourselves, and for your children," Jesus, with complete disregard for his own misery in his great compassion for others, had said on the way to Calvary. Through the years the memory of his broken hands and feet reminded Christians of his infinite love. Jonathan Walker's branded hand became to many Americans symbol of the abolition crusaders' love and charity for the black man, even as Jesus' bleeding wounds proclaimed his devotion to sinful mankind.

By 1845 Americans could bear witness to the abolitionists' acceptance of imprisonment or physical torture as the price of adherence to the cause of the slave. James Burr, Alanson Work, and George Thompson had demonstrated the former by their cheerful resignation to Missouri punishment. Jonathan Walker's branded hand was living proof of the latter. In the next few years still other antislavery men would testify to further parallels between their crusade and the labors of the first evangelists of Christianity.

As
Lambs
Among
Wolves

WHILE Elijah Lovejoy, Prudence Crandall, Theodore Weld, James G. Birney, Alanson Work, James Burr, George Thompson, and Jonathan Walker endured persecution so spectacular that their stories were told and retold from rostrum to rostrum and from journal to journal in abolition circles, dozens of other men took heart from them and joined the antislavery mission. In 1836 the American Anti-Slavery Society chose seventy lecturers to preach abolitionism throughout the North—seventy because it was that number to whom Jesus had said in Biblical days, "Go your ways: behold, I send you forth as lambs among wolves. . . . He that heareth you heareth me. . . ." Theodore Weld gave them intensive training both in public speaking and in abolition lore; he taught them how to make their points and how to defend their contentions; he advised them on ways to avoid physical harm. After three weeks under his inspired tutelage they went out into the land to demonstrate that the abolitionist, even as the apostles of the New Testament, would, for the Negro's deliverance, suffer willingly, unheralded and unhonored.

Of the Seventy, none was more unique in technique or in perseverance than Stephen Symonds Foster. Born in 1809 in Canterbury, New Hampshire, Foster first learned the carpenter's trade, then determined to enter the ministry. He studied first at Dartmouth and then at Union Seminary in New York City. He left the latter place after only a year when he learned that as an ordained minister of the seminary he could not preach abolitionism. When Foster entered the antislavery field he conceived the idea of procuring audiences for his message by entering churches at Sunday-sermon time and claiming the right to instruct the congregations on the obligations of the church to those in bonds in the South.

In September, 1841, Foster first tried his idea in the Old North Church in Concord. He had scarcely begun when three men seized him and whisked him outside. A few months later he came back with what he thought was a surer scheme. From the pew nearest the pulpit he rose at sermon time and asked to speak briefly for two and a half million brethren in bonds in the South. That, quickly replied the minister, would disturb the regular Christian worship. A member of the congregation hurried from the opposite side of the room and seized the intruder by the arm. As the man hustled him down the aisle, the scraggly-bearded Foster asked him calmly if Jesus had ever turned out a man for speaking his mind. His escort did not answer, but instead held his arm more firmly, called to the choir to drown his voice with music, and motioned the sexton to assist with the eviction.

That afternoon Stephen Foster was back, and, despite his friends' pleas that he desist, entered the church as the congregation was gathering. He began at once to address the early arrivals. But church members again evicted him. They kicked him and they pulled his hair; they dragged him down the aisle, then tumbled him down a flight of stairs. His injuries left him bedridden for weeks. Moreover, leaders in the church sued him

for interfering with public worship. At his trial he proved that
the law under which they tried him was no longer in force. But
the judge declared he must pay a five-dollar fine and Foster's
friends rushed to donate the amount. But the disturber declared
the cause of the slave would gain more if he suffered imprisonment. The judge, however, would not permit this. He remitted
the fine and Foster used the money in the cause of the slave.

In 1841 and 1842 Foster and Parker Pillsbury encountered
many mobs as they preached antislavery in New Hampshire. In
Hanover they spent an entire week in efforts to obtain a meeting house before they procured the "dancing room" of the
town hostelry, an environment which would immediately prej-
udice some citizens. At one of the sessions Foster talked on a
resolution which declared that slavery constituted a combination of all man's foulest crimes. "And who perpetrates these
outrages?" he cried. "They are the ministers, bishops . . . presidents and professors of colleges and theological seminaries. . . .
They voluntarily make themselves man-stealers and robbers. . . .
We do not see them do the deeds, and so we hold them innocent. But what would you say if President Lord, of your own college, should be seen carrying home at night a stolen sheep? . . ."[1]
This final question Dartmouth college students present took as
an insult to their college and its president. In answer they
hissed, hooted, whistled, snickered, clapped their hands, and
scraped their feet. Foster stopped talking antislavery, apologized
for what they thought he had said, and expected to continue.
But he could not restore order. Moreover, Hanover would no
longer hear him, and his unfinished lecture marked the end of
the projected series there.

At West Chester, Foster and Pillsbury held an antislavery
meeting and believed everything was well because their small
audience heard them through. But when they went to their
carriage they found that foes had covered buggy seats, reins, and
even their new valises with fetid bovine excrement from a nearby pasture. The following spring an audience in Stratham, New
Hampshire, let Foster get well into a lecture, then quietly left

in a body. He went on to Nashua, arrived on Saturday, and tried
to obtain the use of a meeting house. The best offer he got
came from a minister who permitted him to speak for twenty
minutes in the church vestry. But Foster would be heard further. On Sunday he entered the Baptist church and began to
preach before the regular service. The minister interrupted
him, but Foster paid no attention and continued. A deacon
appeared and dragged him to the street. Foster scrambled up
and tried to re-enter. The deacon blocked the door. Foster
persisted. Suddenly another church member appeared with the
town constable and the three of them carried the offender to
a tavern some distance from the church. They dumped him on
the floor and in a short time the officer had him placed under
guard in an upstairs room. There Foster stayed until his hearing the next morning. When he refused to pay his three-dollar
fine the judge sent him to Amherst jail. But imprisonment
always pleased Foster.

"My enemies never made greater blunder," he wrote from
jail, "than when they sent me to this gloomy prison. It is an
honor I did not expect; one I feared I might never merit. . . .
You and I may be called to yield up our lives in the final
struggle. . . . I have already passed the bitterness of death. My
enemies have done their worst."[2]

On Sunday, June 26, 1842, Foster and two other antislavery
lecturers entered the Congregational church in Lynn and at the
close of the last long prayer of the service Foster began speaking. Two men grabbed him by the shoulders, turned him face
down so a third could hold his feet, and in wheelbarrow fashion
they carried him to the street. In the afternoon he similarly
invaded the Baptist meeting house to begin speaking just as the
service ended. The departing crowd rushed him, some with
such force that he fell to the floor. But with his customary
persistence, he rose and made them a brief speech before he
departed. Later the same day Foster, with his companions, attended a Quaker meeting in Lynn. One of the others interrupted the meditation and some worshippers left in disgust.

Foster quickly seized the opportunity, however, and began to speak to the few who did remain. Several men returned, dragged him halfway to the door, then gave him up to a young Quaker who insisted that he be heard. That evening Foster and one of his companions tried to distribute to members of the Methodist and Baptist churches notices of their six o'clock antislavery meeting. At the latter place some one locked Foster in a closet under the stairway and it was twenty minutes before he could obtain release.

In October, 1842, Foster spoke in the church at Hancock, New Hampshire. At his first words an unruly mob outside clanged the church bell while those inside hooted, hissed, and rolled huge rocks down the main aisle toward the pulpit. Shouting above the noise, Foster managed to continue. But when he criticized a local minister's attitude on slavery, the audience increased the din by sneezing, barking, whistling, and scraping their feet. Soon a man armed with a great club marched in mock solemnity to the altar. With a straight face and much ceremony he seated himself directly before the pulpit. Shortly he marched out, then came back, ascended into the pulpit and began to speak. Foster stopped to hear him. But the crowd seemed not to notice that one of their own talked. Some continued to roll large stones forward. Others shattered the windows, and rocks and flying glass rattled against the pew doors. Someone cried out that the meeting adjourn and the audience scrambled outside as Foster's companion, Parker Pillsbury, shouted after them, "Did your fathers adjourn at Bunker Hill when fired upon by enemies of freedom?"[3] Foster went across the street to the common and again tried to speak. Some who did not want to listen sang psalms to drown his voice and others howled loudly.

Later in 1842 Foster faced a mob in Portland, Maine. As he discussed "The Influence of Southern Slavery in Northern States" the audience began to sing, hiss, hoot, and scream insults. They threw rotten eggs; they dismantled the benches; they started a brawl among themselves. Several rushed for the speaker shouting, "Hand him over! Hand him over! We want the blood of the damned scoundrel. Murder the damned abolitionist." When someone sounded a false alarm of fire, the mobsters, instead of clearing the building, blocked the stairways so that they might lay hands on Foster. As he escaped temporarily, they chased him shouting, "Turn him out; bring a pot of lampblack!" When they caught him, they were merciless as they beat him about the face and head.[4]

In September, 1848, Foster followed Parker Pillsbury as speaker for an antislavery meeting at Harwich, Massachusetts. Although Pillsbury accused a local mariner of accepting a poor slave's money for transportation from Norfolk to some Northern port and of subsequently reporting him for capture, the audience heard the seaman himself defend his actions and remained calm until Foster spoke. After he had uttered only a few sentences concerning the captain's story, a man shouted out that his statements were all lies. The audience rushed at Foster. Some seized a fugitive slave who was present and threw him down behind the platform. Others urged the mariner to do the same to the abolitionist. Rioters surged around Foster and the other speakers on the dais. Fists flew and men with bloodied noses sprawled upon the floor. When it was all over, Foster emerged with painful bruises and clothes nearly torn off.

Stephen S. Foster's tales of his tribulations emphasized the treatment of abolitionists everywhere. He declared that he had been in jail times without number; that churchmen had in one year dragged him from places of worship twenty-four times, had twice thrown him from second-story windows, had seriously injured him; that he had paid fines for preaching the Gospel; that he had been forced to escape assassins; that he had ruined his voice and contracted a lung disease. "Still I will not complain," he wrote, "though death should be found close on my track. My lot is easy compared with that of those for whom I labor."[5] Other antislavery lecturers retold his stories and compared his zeal and perseverance with that of the seventy evangelists Jesus had sent out in Biblical days.

Less colorful than Foster, but with equal enthusiasm for the cause, was Parker Pillsbury of Massachusetts. Born in 1809 in Essex County, Pillsbury became a licensed Congregational minister after study at Andover Theological Seminary. In 1840 he entered the abolition crusade and served first as interim editor of the *Herald of Freedom* at Concord, New Hampshire. When, late in the same year, he took to the lecture platform, his first assigned territory was the state of New Hampshire. His reception there began a long record of persecution.

In November, 1840, a mob at Sanbornton Bridge preceded Pillsbury to the church and coated the pulpit cushions with rotten egg. At the evening session at which he spoke the audience almost succeeded in drowning out his voice. At Dover three ministers who were returning from a church gathering stopped off to attend a Pillsbury-Foster meeting. One offered a resolution that any intelligent person who was not openly engaged in antislavery activity should not be recognized as a Christian. Pillsbury agreed and singled out for criticism a local minister whom he accused of buying and then selling a slave. At this another minister objected that such accusations were made in church and several men defended ministers in general. Pillsbury calmly defended his contention to the former and clarified his original charge for the latter. The audience hissed. Suddenly the place was in darkness. Pillsbury solemnly closed the meeting with prayer, dismissed the assemblage, and groped his way out of the church after them.

At Derry a mob closed in upon the shoemaker shop where Pillsbury and Foster stopped to ask directions. One man shouted that the minister from West Chester had said that the two of them had called his church a brothel. Another shouted, "O, they know what a brothel is," and the crowd roared as the antislavery lecturers got away as best they could. At Franklin, Foster spoke one afternoon and the established minister led his congregation out. During Pillsbury's two-hour evening lecture all went well until young rowdies threw the audience into panic by blowing smoke through holes at the back of the room and talking so boisterously that the listeners had difficulty hearing the speaker. But the audience heard when Pillsbury charged that slaveholders lacked Christianity. Two men moved to strike him. Some demanded an apology for his remarks. Several approached him, and one man said, "Damn you, you have slandered and abused all our ministers and churches, and everything that's good among us."[6] Another seized him by the collar and demanded a retraction of his statements. With Foster's help, however, Pillsbury managed to quiet the critics and he continued. But soon some men left to return shortly with more disturbers and even greater confusion. The town constable declared he had no authority to take the molesters into custody and the abolitionists had to depend upon their own persuasiveness. Combining their efforts, they finally got away to their lodgings.

In 1842, at Salem, Massachusetts, Pillsbury mentioned the deplorable relations of the organized churches with the country's proslavery element and the men in the audience promptly and efficiently dismantled the church. They tore up pews and pulverized the wood; they took down lamps and mutilated shades and reflectors. Frightened women darted about the room and some climbed out the windows to escape the mad activity. Pillsbury narrowly avoided injury.

Parker Pillsbury kept a record of his experiences, and abolitionists recounted his stories in their journals and in their lectures. They pointed out that his valiancy rivaled that of the hallowed ones upon whom Jesus had depended to carry His word and the hope of His Father's kingdom unto all men. Parker Pillsbury, like Stephen S. Foster, had proved himself evangelist and martyr in the likeness of the Biblical Seventy.

But other men, too, were proving themselves worthy of a place beside Foster and Pillsbury in the chronicle of the evangelists of the abolition crusade. One of these was Henry B. Stanton, Connecticut-born descendant of the Separatist leader

William Brewster. Stanton worked in the antislavery field from 1834 until 1846 and could boast of addressing audiences from Indiana to Maine, as well as in Kentucky, Delaware, and Maryland. In the summer of 1832 he made his first antislavery speech at Lane Seminary where he stood alone to deny that the North had any responsibility for assistance to Southern states in quelling slave uprisings. In 1835 an East Greenwich gathering warned him out of town as a vagrant. Shortly thereafter other opponents "honored" him at Newport, Rhode Island, and stoned his lecture building until they smashed all the windows, then entered to drive the listeners into the street. In 1836 in a Methodist church in Providence, group after group from the audience rushed up the aisles as men shook their fists at him and abused him in vile language. After Stanton spoke in Livingston County, New York, residents promptly burned the church in which he had talked. In 1845 a Norwich mob broke every window in the meeting house where he had expected to lecture. He countered by fastening large planks inside the building across the window beside which he was to stand. Thus protected, he successfully completed his lecture series.[7]

Henry B. Stanton claimed the honor of being mobbed in every state in which he spoke, save one. Yet he completed twelve years of effort for the antislavery cause to become an honored evangelizer wherever abolitionists extolled the glory of their crusade for the Negro. Many a man who had sat before him would bear witness that his fortitude and tenacity of purpose surely equalled that of the Biblical Seventy.

While some of the seventy antislavery crusaders—Foster, Pillsbury, Stanton—encountered persecution only slightly less spectacular than that of martyrs like Prudence Crandall, Theodore Weld, James G. Birney, Elijah Lovejoy, and the rest, others could also record brushes with antiabolitionists. Their individual stories broadened the base of the abolition martyr legend even as the tales of the sufferings of the seventy Biblical evangelists fleshened out the Christian tradition of trial by ordeal for those who would spread the teachings of Jesus. Abolitionists eagerly hailed each martyr and solemnly compiled the records of the crusade.

By the mid-1840's the annals included chapters from the experiences of many men. As early as 1830 mobs in Syracuse, New York, attacked Samuel J. May, Harvard graduate and Unitarian clergyman, and burned him in effigy.[8] In 1834 anti-abolitionists in Northfield, New Hampshire, invaded an anti-slavery meeting just as George Storrs began prayer, dragged him from his knees and arrested him as a common brawler. In 1835 Orange Scott, presiding elder and successful Methodist revivalist, spoke in Worcester, Massachusetts. In the midst of his sermon the audience rushed him, destroyed his carefully compiled notes and turned him over to town officers for arrest as a disturber of the peace.[9] In the same year, Amos A. Phelps, Yale graduate who had ministered to Congregational churches in Hopkinton and Boston and won acclaim from abolitionists for defining slavery as the "holding of a human being as property,"[10] faced a brick-throwing mob in Farmington, Connecticut. He stood them out and finished his lecture series.

Several of Theodore Weld's friends from Lane Seminary encountered mobs in his old territory in Ohio. One, James A. Thome, met many during his agency there. In 1836 Canton school directors granted him permission to use the local school for a series of abolition talks. After one lecture, they cancelled the permit and he delivered the other addresses in a small, crowded room. At New Lisbon rioters turned him out of the courthouse after his first discourse. Hanover listeners threw eggs during his lecture but were unable to discourage him. Another Laneite, John W. Alvord, completed a talk in Granville, Ohio, even though opponents demolished the windows, sashes and all, threw in huge stones, and finally covered his companions from head to foot with rotten eggs. They prowled his lodgings and threatened serious damage to his host's home. At Grafton in the same state Sereno W. Streetor, another Lane rebel, finished a lecture series even though a large crowd drummed and piped for the first talk, fired squibs for another, presented him with a wooden horse a third, and promised to climax the whole affair with a coat of tar and feathers for him.[11]

Other abolitionists found martyrdoms in Southern states. In July, 1835, Amos Dresser, former Lane student, went from Cincinnati to Nashville to sell Bibles. City authorities there searched his valises and found antislavery material which he carried for his own reading. They arrested him for distributing incendiary publications, conducted him to the public square, and administered twenty lashes.[12] In the same year Dr. Reuben Crandall, biology instructor in the national capital and brother of Prudence, went to jail on a charge of helping runaway slaves out of the South. Kept in a damp, dungeon-like prison from August, 1835, until the next April, he succumbed to tuberculosis.[13] Every man who suffered brought the abolition movement nearer to a new climax in its turbulent history.

In the decade after Lovejoy, abolitionists expanded the martyr concept and constantly stressed its tradition of willingness to suffer that the Negro might be free. The Alton editor's death climaxed the first phase of the antislavery crusade—a phase rooted in the early opposition of scattered Quakers like Benjamin Lay, John Woolman, Charles Osborn, and Benjamin Lundy, and marked by James G. Birney's quiet logic, Garrison's vituperative emotionalism, and the patient endurance of Prudence Crandall, Theodore Weld, and all the other crusaders. Americans responded to Lovejoy's sacrifice with a spirit which reaffirmed the abolitionists' conviction that one martyrdom converted more men to the cause than could all the lecturers and pamphleteers in two score years. In the ten years after Lovejoy's death antislavery men meditated upon the zeal and selflessness of the early apostles of Christianity. Their reflections renewed their faith and produced new evidence that their devotion to the slave equalled that of the first followers of Jesus. Alanson Work, James Burr, and George Thompson suffered imprisonment like that imposed upon Paul and Silas. Jonathan Walker's endurance of physical torture reminded the faithful that the Master patiently bore his wounds of crucifixion. In addition, seventy men left homes and families to carry abolition fervor to crowds as hostile as any which protested the coming of the same number who in Biblical days, at Jesus' command, set out to evangelize the world. As the post-Lovejoy decade neared its close, abolitionism headed into a new climax.

Of Whom
They Were
Not
Worthy

SHOUTS came from an assembly room of the Maryland capitol in Annapolis one chill January day in 1842. Gathered there were Marylanders who had responded to a call to "all persons favorable to the protection of the slaveholding interests in the state." The abolition movement had created great alarm. Beginning as a mere protest of scattered Puritans and Quakers and a handful of religious people, drawing in strength as Quaker organizations excluded slaveholders and as devout men like Charles Osborn and Benjamin Lundy had organized societies, and then mounting with the work of Garrison and Weld, the antislavery movement had become a potent threat to the slave states.

Especially potent was the propaganda device of martyrdom which the abolitionists used. Elijah Lovejoy, Prudence Crandall, Theodore Weld, James G. Birney, Alanson Work, James E. Burr, George Thompson, and a host of others had suffered persecution for the Negro's freedom. Altogether they had created a great and

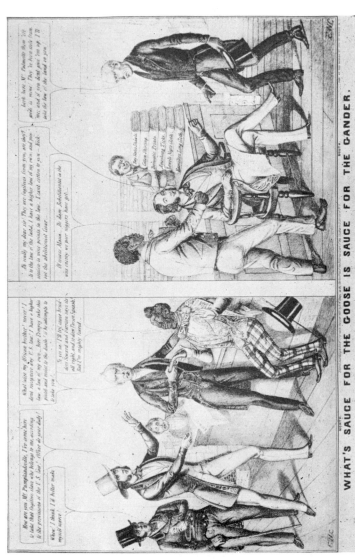

Southern cartoons ridicule abolitionists' efforts to free the slaves (left) and threaten economic reprisal for such efforts (right).

Illustrations from *Parson Brownlow's Book,* a vituperative and colorful account of Brownlow's stand against secession. *Above:* He enters the Knoxville jail. *Below:* Southern barbarity illustrated. He vowed in prison to make this engraving.

powerful force so that the movement which had been just another organizational one had the fire of a crusade. The strength of the agitation had been so great that in Maryland the slaveholders were moved to take steps to protect themselves. The men who assembled in Annapolis that day had no intention of adding another name to the growing honor roll of freedom. They had assembled solely to consult together.

But their anger was aroused by the presence of a young reporter from Massachusetts with a notebook. He claimed the privilege of reporting the convention for several Northern journals whose Washington correspondent he was. Rumor, however, had convinced the slaveholders that he was an abolitionist and would report their doings according to his own views on the slavery question. In a committee room near the convention hall sat the young reporter, awaiting admittance to the larger room. Anger flared as members debated whether or not to admit him, and some men advanced menacingly toward the Northerner.

Object of their anger was Charles Turner Torrey, minister and antislavery editor. Already known to many as an anti-Garrison abolitionist, Torrey had previously proved that he had the courage to defend his strong antislavery convictions. Born at Scituate November 21, 1813, he spent his childhood with his indulgent grandparents. He prepared for Yale at Phillips Academy and during his first year of college attended a revival series which led him to resolve to lead the true Christian life, to become God's disciple. His youthful instability and lack of perseverance—probably a result of his grandparents' laxity in training him—reduced the effectiveness of his high resolve and after three years and graduation at Yale, he yet had little idea of what he would do with his life. In November, 1833, however, he began teaching the local school in West Brookfield, Massachusetts. His troubles there, he concluded, stemmed "either in my ignorance of human nature, or in want of self-control, which is never taught, except at home."[1]

So Torrey was not content to teach. In addition to his troubles with the children, his financial worries, occasioned not only by the recklessness with which he had spent a patrimony left him by his grandfather, but also by his extensive borrowing for school expenses and the purchase of a considerable library, made him preoccupied and irritable. In 1834, as he prepared to quit the classroom, he wrote, "My mind has been occupied, anxiously so, with the difficulties and discouragements of my situation. It has affected my countenance and my feelings, and so unfitted me for the duties of my station."[2] Then he hearkened again to the resolve made at Yale. He would enter the ministry.

In 1834 Torrey enrolled in the theological seminary at Andover. But again his intentions met delay. Within the year poor health forced him to request dismissal. He believed he suffered from tuberculosis, the disease of which both his parents had died. On his physician's advice he took a long pedestrian journey and within a few months resumed his studies, this time training with established ministers. During 1835 and 1836 he worked with the Reverend L. A. Spofford of Scituate, assisted a minister of Cohasset in a revival, and finally completed his preparation with the Reverend Jacob Ide of West Medway. On October 25, 1836, the Mendon Association of Congregational Ministers licensed Charles Torrey to preach.

In the next months, as Torrey looked around for a ministerial appointment, he found that growing antislavery agitation had brought cleavage to many congregations. "My abolition*ism* and Emmons*ism*," he wrote early in 1837 when he desired placement in Providence, "might cause a few to leave, and would draw others. The friends of the slave are determined to have one abolition church, and the abolitionists are the sound men in doctrine. Still, something may occur to cause a struggle and prevent my remaining here."[3] The following month he accepted a call to the Richmond Street Congregational Church in Providence.

With his bride, Mary Ide, daughter of his ministerial tutor, Torrey established himself in his new position and turned his attention not only to the immediate problems of his congregation, but also to the great moral issues of the day. Little by little, he found himself more occupied with the latter and his discourses turned more and more to the evils of the American slave system. In January, 1838, he accepted a call to the Harvard Street Church in Salem where George Barrell Cheever had already abolitionized the congregation.

But Torrey grew restless ministering to those who were already converted to abolition. In 1839 he joined the anti-Garrison forces in the Massachusetts Anti-Slavery Society and campaigned for a paper to replace the *Liberator*. With a number of other ministers, he contended that Garrison discussed too many extraneous matters: peace, Sabbath observance, nonresistance, the injustices of human government, and women's rights. At the final division in the society Garrison broadcast Torrey's name wherever the *Liberator* went, for he believed him the leader of the opposition to him and his paper. When Torrey became editor of the new Massachusetts Abolition Society's publication, the *Massachusetts Abolitionist,* Garrison inaugurated a new series of editorial blasts. By 1840 Torrey's battles with the Garrisonites in the national society over the matter of turning the antislavery crusade into a political movement made his name increasingly familiar to American abolitionists.

In the course of this work Charles Torrey crystallized his over-all abolition program. He would evangelize the slaveholders, while at the same time teaching the slaves to read the Bible. "A few more Lovejoys might fall;" he said, "but the yoke of slavery would be broken; for we should see that slavery could not endure *pure* Christianity."[4] Further, abolition societies must provide more speakers for public lecture tours; the press must enlarge its appeal; clergymen must convince Christians of the sin involved in slave-keeping; and finally, all abolitionists must promote the use of the right of petition and of the franchise. He hoped also to identify slavery, which he believed violated both church and public law, with the vilest of crimes, so that eventually even the courts would be antislavery.

"When the 'opinions' of the MASSACHUSETTS public are right," Torrey wrote, "we expect the legislative, judicial, and executive powers will be wielded, so far as may be, in favor of liberty and against slavery. When the majority of the NATIONAL 'public' are right, CONGRESS will sweep away every vestige of slavery within the limits of its constitutional power. Separate states will, one by one, do the same; and so on, till the work is done."[5]

But Torrey was not content with this mild, long-range program. He turned to more active means of aiding the Negro to freedom. In 1841 he brought a Boston seaman into court for his insistence upon returning to the South a stowaway North Carolina fugitive slave. Abolition journals carefully reported the incident and praised Torrey. His action and the subsequent publicity, however, did not save the runaway from return to bondage. It did occasion the organization of the Boston Vigilance Committee to secure to colored persons their constitutional and legal rights. Torrey became secretary for the group.[6] But his financial troubles grew steadily worse. Neither as a minister nor as an abolitionist editor and lecturer could he support his family. He determined to try a new career and in late 1841 went to Washington as correspondent for a number of New York and Boston papers.[7] He was attending to his duties in this capacity in January, 1842, when he ran into trouble in the slaveholders' convention in Annapolis.

At the Thursday evening session of the convention in the state capitol on January 12 Torrey had just begun to take notes for his report to his papers when the chairman asked that all nonmembers leave the room. When other reporters remained, Torrey hesitated. Then John M. S. Causin, brilliant young Annapolis attorney, moved that nonmembers be allowed seats on the floor only through sponsorship by an accredited dele- also currently reporting. After adjournment, he decided, he gate. Torrey knew no one, but assumed that the rule functioned as it did for the United States Congress whose sessions he was would introduce himself to some delegate and for the remaining sessions would procure a better vantage point on the floor. So he found a place among the gallery spectators and continued with his note-taking. But almost immediately the doorkeeper appeared and ordered him to leave the building. Quickly he gathered up his belongings and started out with the messenger. Suddenly the man seized him by the collar and ordered him into a committee room to await the convention's decision on whether or not to admit him. Torrey at first objected, then yielded when the doorkeeper said that the group would doubtless let him in soon.

For some time thereafter Torrey heard the slaveholders' disagreement over him as Causin presented to them the question of his admittance. Their debate was heated. Finally the angriest of the Southerners left the main hall and came threateningly into the committee room. Many reviled him; a few urged him to leave town.

Finally Torrey agreed to return to Washington. But before he could start on his way, a mob waylaid him, followed him to his lodgings and insisted that he settle his account there at once. Then the leaders surged into his room to rummage through his papers as they protested loudly against abolitionists. When they could find nothing that substantiated their accusations, they still argued whether or not they should let such an incendiary go in peace. Some threatened tar and feathers. Some wanted him hanged. Others urged that he leave town at once. But even as they talked, a clerk arrived to present Torrey with a magistrate's warrant which committed him to jail. As the officer hurried him along, the mob followed, some protesting slow legal processes as a means of dealing with hated abolitionists. Then for three days Torrey shivered and prayed among imprisoned slaves in Annapolis jail. In the dampness and cold of his unheated cell he rededicated his life to the emancipation of the Negro.

"May God help me to be faithful," he said later, "to that *pledge made in Annapolis jail*. In that cell, God helping me, if it stands, I will celebrate the emancipation of the slaves in Maryland before ten years more roll away."[7]

Outside the bleak walls news of Torrey's arrest spread. On Monday, as the hour of trial drew near, the courtroom bulged with spectators. Some came of curiosity, for it was not often they viewed a man who risked his freedom and his life in an unpopular cause; some came to see a wretch flogged, tarred and feathered, even hanged. Others hoped to blast the name of Torrey with a denunciation which would damn every abolitionist in the land.

At eleven o'clock Judge Nicholas Brewer called Torrey for hearing. John M. S. Causin, whose keen mind and forceful voice had already won him political recognition, acted for the state. Confidently he examined witnesses against Torrey—witnesses whose jaundiced testimony evinced more hatred than facts. Casting aside any doubt as to Torrey's abolitionism, Causin read from extreme antislavery journals and interpreted his brief convention notes in their light. He emphasized the baseness of the groups whose agent he said Torrey was; he branded him an incendiary and a disseminator of dangerous doctrines. The crowd cheered.

But Torrey's counsel, Thomas S. Alexander, Maryland antislavery man, replied only briefly to Causin's remarks, then asked his client to take the stand. After Torrey answered routine questions, Judge Brewer declared that he must retain him until the court could investigate statements which some state witnesses testified that Torrey had attributed to Maryland Negroes. As Judge Brewer signed the commitment which remanded him to jail for another week, Torrey well knew how serious would be his predicament if the court should later find him guilty of plotting with Negroes against the laws of Maryland. But when Torrey went again before Judge Brewer, the slaveholders' convention had dispersed, popular excitement had subsided, and he secured release upon bond to keep the peace. His sufferings had not been great, but abolition journals had already spread his story through the North.

Torrey returned to his writing, did some lecturing, and in the fall of 1842 went to Albany to spend a year as editor of an anti-Garrison paper, the *Tocsin of Liberty,* mouthpiece of the political abolitionists. Then in 1843 he again clashed with the slavocracy. Well on his way to become a martyr for abolitionism, Torrey looked for opportunity to immolate himself on the altars of his cause. Soon a Negro who had successfully traveled the underground railway to Canada appealed for his help in getting his wife and children out of slavery's chains. Torrey readily agreed and hastened South with the man. At the Pennsylvania border he hired a span of horses and a carriage and traveled into the national capital to meet the fugitives. But before he could execute his plan police officers seized the Negro family and the horses and vehicle. Hastily Torrey sent to friends and borrowed money to pay for animals and carriage. Then he went on to Delaware and worked with the underground railroad. In a short time he returned North and in Philadelphia met one Emily Webb, a free Negro, who asked him to bring out of bondage her husband and children, slaves of Bushrod Taylor in Virginia. This Torrey did, then returned North.

Early in 1844 Torrey, whose financial difficulties were ever with him, moved to Baltimore and made plans for going into the starch manufacturing business. But before he could start operations and bring his family South, he was again in trouble over the laws against aiding fugitive slaves to escape. On June 24 an executive requisition from Virginia sent him to the Baltimore jail for his part in the Webb family escape the previous year. Immediately one William Heckrotte of Baltimore signed a warrant for his detention for aiding certain slaves of his out of Maryland. Since the Webb case involved extradition to Virginia, Heckrotte's charge took precedence and Maryland authorities kept Torrey in jail to await trial.

By this time Charles Turner Torrey well knew the value of his persecution to the abolition cause. He got the Baltimore *Patriot* to let his friends know of his arrest and imprisonment. On July 29 he wrote to abolitionists of Essex County, Massachusetts, and joyfully invited them to meet him around Washington's monument in Baltimore on July 4, 1848, to celebrate the triumph of liberty in Maryland. Three days later he sent the president of the same meeting a letter in which he explained his situation and defended his actions, then launched into detailed observations concerning the wise use of political power as a means of ending slavery. He must keep his name before interested groups. In a letter to Boston colored people who held a sympathy meeting for him, he defended himself against other abolitionists who criticized his methods of aiding the Negro, making much of the point that he suffered imprisonment only because Maryland law made acts of common humanity illegal. On August 30 he ran an advertisement in the *Baltimore Sun* in which he explained his slave-running activities and denied both that he had done wrong and that he courted sympathy. Then he considered the primary issues involved in charges lodged against him. He set aside as inconsequential the question of his guilt in aiding the escape of slaves belonging to citizens of either Virginia or Maryland. The charge against him concerned the infringement of hard-won American constitutional guarantees.[8]

"What are the legal issues?" he wrote. "1. One is not peculiar to my case. It is, whether a mere requisition from the authorities of another State, unsupported by evidence of the commission of any crime, or of the identity of the person, shall be deemed sufficient warranty to drag a man from his home, his family, his friends, into a foreign jurisdiction, to be tried by strangers. If so, we have gained little by the revolution of 1776. 2. The second issue is, is it 'felony or other crime,' within the meaning of the constitution of the United States, to aid a slave to escape to a free state? The *local* laws of one half of even the SLAVE States do not make it so. 3. Has SLAVERY any constitutional or legal existence in Maryland or Virginia? or does it exist by mere sufferance . . . ? 4. Is it a *crime* at all, by the law of God, by the common law, or the constitutions of Maryland and Virginia, to help a man out of slavery? If not, can a mere local statute law *make* it so? Can laws make acts of humanity and mercy to the helpless and poor become *crimes* by the words written on a parchment and signed by officials?"[9]

While denying aspiration to martyrdom before the public, Torrey wrote his wife: "If I am to suffer, it is a great consolation to know that it will not be in vain; that Providence will use even my sufferings to overthrow, more speedily, the accursed system that enslaves and degrades so many millions of the poor of our land. So in *that* I do, and I will rejoice. Shall a man be put into the Penitentiary for doing good?—for doing his plain duty to the poor and oppressed?"[10]

Abolition groups adopted Torrey's cause. On August 26 colored people in Boston held a sympathy meeting and resolved that his imprisonment was inconsistent with inalienable rights and that his friends should contribute money for his assistance. A public meeting in Upton, Massachusetts, declared sympathy for him, called upon all abolitionists to support him, and took up a collection for his relief. At Northampton citizens met to pray for Torrey and Jonathan Walker and urged the importance of prompt action in behalf of the former. They brought in a Negro purported to be a Torrey accomplice and heard his story. The abolition journals faithfully reported these and many more meetings and added requests from readers that still others be held. Torrey's case was familiar to a large number of Americans long before the day of his trial.

But while he waited, Torrey again became the subject of disagreement among his abolition brethren. After only a few weeks in jail the prisoner, never a robust man, became ill. He had at first hoped that since two states wanted him on similar charges his case might go to a federal court. But he believed that in order to get a hearing before the federal court he would have to give two thousand dollars bail. Despite the sympathy of many abolitionists, many others thought him foolish and all through the hot summer he faced disappointment that no one raised the money for him. The longer he stayed in jail and the weaker he became the more he despaired of facing a Southern jury. Unfortunately, on September 13 he attempted escape. With the help of his cell mates he had made considerable headway in sawing through the bars with improvised tools when the prison officers discovered the plan. Once again abolition circles buzzed with contrary views of Torrey's action. Some damned the slave system for fostering a situation in which a humanitarian lay ill in a miserable jail for aiding the helpless; some called him rash; some inquired for his professed willingness to suffer for the cause. When his trial began in November, friends and foes alike still debated.

The outcome of the trial was never in doubt and abolitionists knew it. They could not save Torrey, but they could exploit his martyrdom for the cause. The indictment charged that he enticed, persuaded, and assisted certain of William Heckrotte's slaves to escape. On December 1 he received sentence of six years in the penitentiary, and a month later he began a prison term which would continue until April 2, 1851. Abolition forces spread his story over the land.

Even before his sentence, Torrey's supporters had started a "martyr fund" for him. The abolition journals carried continual announcements on the growth of the fund and urged more donations. Some money would be used for Torrey's own expenses and the rest for the relief of his family, for the little which Mrs. Torrey could earn by her writing for small journals, even when added to help from personal friends, could barely provide for her and the two children. On January 13, 1845, the *Emancipator* announced that even the "old organization" antislavery men were collecting money. The same paper published a list of letters and announcements to encourage donations. In addition, all other antislavery organs published their own lists of contributors and amounts.

Antislavery groups publicized expressions of sympathy for Torrey. On December 23, 1844, the Buffalo city antislavery society adopted ten resolutions declaring that his act was not criminal and expressing sympathy for his family. The same week Boston abolitionists held a dinner meeting and heard

Joseph C. Lovejoy, John Pierpont, and Nathaniel P. Colver praise Torrey and condemn Maryland law. On January 3, 1845, after weeks of cautiously refraining from committing himself, Garrison admitted that he could excuse Torrey for his imprudence. The *Emancipator and Chronicle* suggested publication of a book titled *Letters from Prison*. It could contain a selection of letters and papers which Torrey wrote while in Baltimore jail as well as the *Defence* which his counsel read before the court to point out perjury in the testimony of witnesses who helped convict him. If friends who had received other than business letters from him would send them, these, too, might be published. Abolition journals faithfully carried stories of his life in prison: how he worked on the warping machine, when he was ill, what books he received, how many visitors came. On June 18 the *Emancipator and Chronicle* reported that a correspondent had visited Torrey and that he enjoyed good health, opportunities for reading, good food, a clean sleeping room, light labors, the privilege of attending worship, and time to write letters for himself and for his fellow prisoners. But, said the informant, there was *no prospect* of his release. Meanwhile, he was an excellent religious influence over the other inmates. The same paper published a five-verse Torrey lament on conditions for liberty in the United States. In November the paper urged its readers to "Remember Torrey at the polls."

In the fall of 1845 Torrey's health failed. Visitors reported that his eyes were dim, his voice hoarse, his body emaciated, his movements feeble, and his spirits extremely depressed. He would surely die, they said, unless his family and friends could secure his release so that he could get proper care.[11]

Both groups went into action at once. Early in 1845 Mrs. Torrey's father, Reverend Jacob Ide, had investigated the possibilities for obtaining a pardon from the governor of Maryland. In April Mrs. Torrey had reported to her husband that if he would promise never to "go to those States FOR THAT PURPOSE AGAIN"[12] certain influential members of the Senate would probably petition for the pardon. Even Massachusetts' chief executive would petition for him. Torrey would not promise. So it was nearly a year later that his friends again began to work out plans for his release. In January, 1846, Amos A. Phelps went south for an interview with the Maryland governor. He accomplished nothing. All he learned was that Torrey would die unless he left the prison very soon. The papers reported details of a circular and letter which Mrs. Torrey sent to the governor. She explained that her husband did assist runaway slaves, but said he had not coaxed them away. She regretted that he took counsel with his feelings instead of with his judgment and concluded that the senators from Massachusetts, and two ex-governors of the state backed her in her pleas. "I feel authorized," she wrote, "to give the fullest assurance, both to you and the people of Maryland, that my husband will never visit your State for that purpose."[13] Friends added statements that Torrey's efforts were entirely unconstitutional, that they and the North generally disapproved of such actions, but that they, members of the Massachusetts legislature and of the state's courts, would assure Maryland that if he were released he would not repeat his offenses. In March Amos A. Phelps sent to the governor of Maryland a duplicate of a letter originally sent the previous August, asking if Torrey could be released without dishonorable concessions, what concessions he might have to make, how much money he would need, and inquiring if release from Maryland would automatically excuse him on the Virginia charge. Shortly Phelps announced that he thought he had arranged for Torrey's freedom for a stated amount of money to pay counsel and court costs. On November 21, 1845, he engaged an attorney for Torrey and three days later said he hoped to effect release in two or three weeks. Again the negotiations dragged along, for the authorities would not promise that release in Maryland would not mean immediate extradition for trial in the Webb case. In addition, Heckrotte had lost interest in Torrey's paying for his slaves because he thought the state legislature was about to reimburse him for the loss. By March, 1846, the negotiations had become so involved and

Torrey's health so impaired that his agents withdrew the offer of payment and determined to use the money for his family after his certain death.[14]

Meanwhile, the abolition periodicals continued publicity on his case. The *Liberator* announced that a book by Torrey, *Home, or the Pilgrim's Faith Revived,* would soon be ready for sale. It would chronicle the decline and revival of spiritual religion in a Puritan church. It would feature scenes and incidents from Torrey's childhood home. All the journals gave running bulletins on the state of his health and noted the requests made upon the Maryland governor for his release. Garrison said that Torrey should rather die in jail than secure dismissal on such humiliating terms as those suggested by his friends and family. When the Baltimore *Visitor* announced the withdrawal of what the abolitionists were calling "ransom money" for Torrey's freedom, it also said that the prisoner was writing for publication a tale called *The Dead Heart.*[15] One editor quoted a reader: "It appears that Charles Torrey is to be a *third* martyr in the great antislavery struggle. The blood of Lovejoy stains the streets of Alton, *Mahan* has been sent home to enjoy communion with Jesus Christ, the great 'Liberator,' and *Torrey* is pining away in a Penitentiary, with no hope of deliverance, until death shall break his fetters, and loosen the iron grasp of the *merciless despots.*"[16] What is wrong, the paper asked, with Torrey's friends, North as well as South, that no one rescues him?

Early in April, 1846, report came that Torrey was sinking rapidly. He was so ill that prison authorities had sent him to the hospital. Abolitionists reiterated their demands for his release, that he might die in peace. Some lamented Mrs. Torrey's inability to visit her husband because she herself was ill. A *Liberator* reader wrote Garrison that ours was a "guilty nation," guilty of Torrey's "slow, fiendlike murder." By the end of the month Torrey's family and friends knew that he could live only a few days.[17]

In Boston, on May 2, a Torrey committee called some forty

people to a meeting of a "few friends" at Marlboro Chapel. They would consider what funeral solemnities were in order, make arrangements for Torrey's burial in Mount Auburn cemetery, consider the purchase of a suitable monument, and discuss what provision might be made for his family. Members of his church sent their pastor to visit the sick man, and to administer communion. The clergyman reported Torrey in the last stages of tuberculosis. Is ours a free land, queried the *Cincinnati Chronicle,* when a man like Torrey dies for a principle? Other newspapers reported visits by friends or sympathizers. Ministers announced they would offer special prayers for the prisoner.[18] Henry B. Stanton published a letter in which Torrey had written, "If I am a guilty man, I am a very guilty one; for, I have aided nearly *Four Hundred* slaves to escape to freedom, the greater part of whom would probably, but for my exertions, have died in slavery." Posterity, said Stanton, would do justice to "our fallen friend." He may be called rash, Stanton added, but if the world had never seen any imprudence, would it have seen any change?[19]

When Torrey died on May 9, 1846, newspaper reaction ran from simple announcements of his death to elaborate descriptions of the funeral. Some said more about the wickedness of the slave power than they did about Torrey's sacrifice. An Illinois woman wrote that she thought the people of Baltimore rejoiced in his death. A Hartford editor classed him with LaFayette. Another man thanked God that Torrey was at last out of "worse than pirate hands." Sympathetic editors draped their pages in heavy black lines and presented the story under large headlines. Over and over editors called him "martyr." The Wisconsin *Freeman* said, "God remembers his prayers and efforts, and in his own time will respond to the cry of his martyred ones, 'O Lord, how long dost thou not avenge our blood?'" Abolition papers received reams of poetry and published much of it.[20]

The Boston committee made all arrangements for Torrey's funeral and abolitionist editors reported every detail. They described the embalming method and the "neat cherry coffin" lined with zinc, in which a pane of glass was of great comfort to friends and relatives who wanted a last look at the martyr. So Torrey came home to a carefully planned ceremony scheduled for Park Street Church. But a few hours before the services the committee received a curt note from the trustees declaring that the edifice would not be available. They scurried about and shortly had permission to use Tremont Temple.

For the crowd which attended the funeral, abolition ministers of several denominations conducted services. Preceding the rites, the body lay in state for three hours. As the ritual began, each pastor offered prayer. Then the Reverend Joseph C. Lovejoy of Cambridgeport, brother of the fallen Elijah, took his text from the eighteenth verse of the one-hundred-fifth psalm: "Whose feet they hurt with fetters: he was laid in iron." In developing the theme, he reviewed all the troubles which had come to Torrey because of his resolve to work for the freedom of the Negro. As the mourners, amongst whom were many clergymen from the surrounding region and a number of Negroes, filed silently out to enter their carriages or to go afoot with the procession to Mount Auburn cemetery, friends stood at the door to accept contributions for the distressed widow and her children.[21]

So Torrey was no more, but his story was the most sensational for the antislavery crusade since Lovejoy's death nine years before. Indeed, some months before he died one admirer had written to a friend in Baltimore, "You have in your city a martyr to this cause—*Charles T. Torrey*. I know him personally—and a noble spirit he is. . . . Yet he is now imprisoned in one of the *Republican* (?) states of this Union for the crime of carrying out in practice what he then proclaimed with every man's assent—*the Equality of man*. Maryland will yet blush at this Deed! I would rather be the Felon—Charles T. Torrey—than the highest and most powerful of his oppressors. Posterity, if the present generation should not do him justice, will vindicate his memory and enrol his name among Freedom's Noble Martyrs!"[22] In many ways, Torrey's experience was of more use than that of the Alton martyr, for it was not so easily befogged with the question of whether he fell for antislavery or for some constitutional right, as the Lovejoy affair had become entangled with freedom of speech and press; it had dragged out a long time before the dramatic climax of his death in the Maryland jail. Charles Turner Torrey had joined the martyrs fallen in the fight against slavery.

After the martyr's death, Americans held dozens of Torrey meetings. The day before his funeral, citizens met in Assonet Village and in Boston. On the burial evening Henry B. Stanton spoke at St. Paul's Church in Lowell and collected money for the Torrey fund. At the same time a Charlestown, Massachusetts, audience heard a minister eulogize Torrey. For some weeks after his death Joseph C. Lovejoy repeated a funeral sermon to as many eastern congregations as would hear him. Torrey's own minister gave a public account of his visit with the martyr during his last days. A meeting in Bangor, Maine, declared Torrey a martyr to the laws of a professedly Christian state. On May 16, a week after Torrey's death, Salmon P. Chase presided at a huge meeting in Cincinnati. Resolutions there condemned Maryland's treatment and sent a message of condolence to the widow. The *Emancipator* presented the suggestion of an Ohio man that a day, preferably July 4, be set aside as one on which people all over the North would assemble to hear funeral discourses or orations in honor of the martyred Torrey. On May 18 Boston staged a meeting in Faneuil Hall. General Samuel Fessenden of Maine presided, and Ellis Gray Loring, Francis Jackson, and John G. Whittier assisted with details. Besides Fessenden, Henry B. Stanton, Walter Channing, and Joseph C. Lovejoy addressed the meeting. Negroes at Oberlin College adopted Torrey resolutions, as did a white group near Salem, Ohio. Ministers in Springfield, Massachusetts, held commemoration meetings for him. Abolitionists in Galesburg, Illinois, adopted resolutions of approval of his actions. A Connecticut minister delivered a funeral discourse at the annual meeting of the state antislavery society and then repeated it to his own congregation. On June 15 Boston Negroes met to declare that Torrey had died on the altar of American slavery and pledged that they would live in the memory of his name. On June 28 the Reverend Dennis Harris addressed an audience in black-draped King Street Wesleyan Chapel. The name of Torrey, he said, should henceforth strike terror into the hearts of oppressors. A few days later the Reverend Lucius C. Matlack preached a Torrey funeral sermon for Boston Methodists. Other ministers throughout New England preached similarly; some published their work in pamphlets and presented them for sale. On July 19 a church group in Clockville, New York, followed a résumé of Torrey's life and work with the singing of a hymn which the composer entitled "Torrey's Grave." The same month Alvan Stewart wept for the martyr as he spoke before the American and Foreign Anti-Slavery Society. When he addressed the annual meeting of the New England Anti-Slavery Society, Parker Pillsbury praised Torrey and condemned Northern lethargy. Boston, however, climaxed all the Torrey meetings with a tremendous celebration on July 31, at a time when Joseph Lovejoy was giving his funeral sermon in other parts of New England. As the ceremonies started, a brass band led a procession through the city to one of the churches, then on to Tremont Temple. Men carried banners which depicted a narrative of slavery against liberty. At Tremont Temple speakers addressed the citizens and all joined in a discussion of the Torrey story. The audience enjoyed a "social interchange of thought and sentiment" and partook of refreshments. As the clocks struck midnight, one of the ministers led the people in prayer before they departed for their homes.

During those same weeks after Torrey's death the fund committee collected money for the family and for a suitable monument. Subscribers could indicate for which purpose they were contributing. Collectors worked in various communities in New England and farther west. Boston friends even employed the Reverend Hiram Cummings to spend a short period devoted entirely to the Torrey collection in the vicinity of that city. Abolition groups turned over to the fund all monies collected at the annual Independence Day antislavery programs. By mid-July the committee had collected over sixteen hundred dollars and was sending out request cards to be returned with money by early fall.[23]

It was a long time before the Torrey excitement abated. In January, 1849, Wendell Phillips, in reviewing Boston's local antislavery history, said: "Where is Park Street? Refusing to receive within its walls, for funeral services, the body of the only martyr the orthodox Congregationalists of New England have had, Charles T. Torrey, and of whom they were not worthy."[24] Henceforth abolition orators extolled two men who had achieved complete martyrdom for the cause: Elijah Parish Lovejoy and Charles Turner Torrey.

In the decade after Elijah Lovejoy's death, abolitionism had moved toward a new climax. The persecution of the imprisoned James E. Burr, Alanson Work, and George Thompson in Missouri, of the tortured Jonathan Walker in Florida, of the much mobbed Stephen S. Foster, Parker Pillsbury, Henry B. Stanton, and others of the evangelizing antislavery Seventy in several states, brought a foreboding expectancy to the movement. The time had come for a new break in the stormy narrative of abolition. Torrey's death brought that climax to the second decade of the militant antislavery crusade. He had once rejoiced that his sufferings might further the slaves' cause. But he could never know how much more agitation there would be nor how many more martyrs would fall before the American Negro would go free.

Appeal To Ballot And Statute

AMERICAN abolitionists by 1850 had accomplished more than the contribution of two martyrs actually fallen in the cause of the slave. For the movement had needed not only publicity but also recognition as a reputable crusade. The sufferings of all the martyrs, and particularly the sacrifice of Lovejoy and Torrey, accomplished the former; attainment of the latter necessitated associating abolitionism with concepts already accepted as cherished American traditions. At this task the crusaders worked zealously.

When in the early eighteen-thirties abolitionists first presented their doctrine of immediate emancipation and mobs stoned their speakers and destroyed their publishing offices, the crusaders reminded Americans of the constitutional guarantees of freedom of speech and of the press. These rights, they declared, were revered by Americans, and were due even to those with whom a majority disagreed. Again challenged by mobs as they organized local, state, and national societies to spread their doctrines, abolitionists stood upon their right of peaceable assembly and went ahead. Subsequently they met other forms of opposition and made common cause with other civil rights.

Shortly after its organization in 1833 the American Anti-Slavery Society engaged in a dispute over the constitutional right of petition. In addition to their work of organizing anti-slavery groups and distributing abolitionist publications, the agents of the national association collected and forwarded to Congress thousands of signatures to petitions which requested that body to act against American slavery. Although every Congress had received such petitions, it was not until 1835 that Southerners protested against them as serious threats to the very foundation of the South's economy. In the following year, they maneuvered the adoption of the first of the gag rules, which, until 1844, with neither printing, reference to committee, nor any discussion, tabled all petitions relating to any phase of the slavery question. But abolitionists quickly turned the gags to advantage. Enlisting every available worker and agent and making use of every means to obtain signatures, they flooded Congress with antislavery petitions. They asked for the abolition of slavery in the District of Columbia and of all domestic slave trade, for a law prohibiting slavery in the territories, for the repeal of the gag rules and for the rejection of both the annexation of Texas and of the admission of additional slave states. John Quincy Adams, who saw in the gags the violation of a vital right, presented petition after petition to the House of Representatives; John C. Calhoun and other Southerners fought to forestall them as likely to invite agitation over slavery. But abolitionists commanded the situation. They sent in more petitions, dispatched Theodore Weld to Washington to assemble antislavery materials for Adams' use, and loudly proclaimed that Southern willingness to annul established rights in order to protect slavery would shortly lead to the shelving of other constitutional guarantees. Men who hearkened not to pleas for the slave rallied to defend abolitionist insistence upon the retention of rights which the Constitution assured white Americans.

At the same time, abolitionists also battled over use of the postal service. In the South, men had frequently demanded that antislavery pamphlets and newspapers be barred from the mails. Such demands, however, remained local until the matter came before Congress and the nation when citizens of Charleston, South Carolina, took action. There, in July, 1835, a mob forcibly entered the post office, seized and burned abolition pamphlets as "incendiary." When Postmaster General Amos Kendall did not censure the deed and President Andrew Jackson subsequently included in his annual message to Congress a request for a national law to stop the circulation of such publications, and Calhoun demanded that local postmasters be given authority to judge and to refuse delivery of incendiary matter, abolitionists grasped pens and mounted rostrums. The guarantees of the Constitution, they wrote and they shouted, belonged to all Americans. The right to send materials uncensored through the mails extended even to minority groups. Indeed, declared the Executive Committee of the American Anti-Slavery Society, the postmaster general and the president had condemned the tenets of their organization on the basis of biased reports and upon hearsay. Was this procedure, they queried, in accord with the revered American principle that men are innocent until proved guilty? When civil officers could censor the mails to protect slavery, Southerners would soon demand censorship of speech, the press, perhaps even morals and religion if some Americans adopted moral or religious beliefs which frowned upon the Negro's bondage.

Into each of these conflicts the abolitionists' status as martyrs for freedom fitted to perfection. Challenged in their exercise of the rights of free speech, free press, to assemble, to petition the government, to use the mails to propagate minority sentiments, they not only were quick to recognize violations of basic rights, but they also displayed both the conviction and the courage to maintain their stand. Solemnly they called upon all Americans to join them in the quest for the American ideal in civil and human rights. So with every struggle the abolition crusade edged into greater respectability.

With the slavery question thus before Congress and the

nation after 1835, the abolitionists late in the decade divided over the future course of their efforts. On one side the Garrisonians argued that the movement should continue the moral crusade and on the other the political abolitionists contended that only recourse to the ballot would rid the country of the hated institution. In 1840 the two groups separated and each went about the work of abolition according to its particular beliefs.

In that year, the political abolitionists quickly organized a party upon a platform which called for the abolition of slavery in the District of Columbia and of all domestic slave trade and announced that they would work for the eventual abolition of slavery in every state. Against the Democrat Martin Van Buren and the Whig William Henry Harrison, the new Liberty Party offered for the presidency of the United States, James G. Birney, Kentucky slaveholder turned abolitionist. But antislavery speeches went unheard in a noisy campaign which lauded Van Buren's fine record in public office and extolled the value of Harrison's log cabin background. Birney polled but seven thousand votes.

Despite this poor showing, the party four years later again nominated Birney against the Whigs' Henry Clay and the Democrats' James K. Polk. Although defeated, the Liberty Party polled 62,000 ballots and some politicians credited it with drawing enough votes from Clay in New York to throw that state, and with it the election, to proslavery Polk. But in the campaign the party had nullified its own future, for its speakers had argued that the effects of the panic of 1837 were really due to the incompatibility of slavery and prosperity. The return of good times after 1844 belied their contention. Consequently by 1848 Liberty Party men faced the necessity for a realignment and a restatement of the tenets of political abolitionism.

Meanwhile, within a few days of Torrey's death in May, 1846, the United States and Mexico finally went to war over the Texas boundary dispute. Antislavery men charged that the war was but a Southern conspiracy to gain additional slave area, and David Wilmot of Pennsylvania made his initial introduction of the proviso which would forbid slavery in any territory acquired from Mexico. Americans thus had four possible solutions to the question of the extension of slavery into the territories. They could accept Wilmot's suggestion, they could follow the South's insistence upon complete noninterference by either Congress or the state legislatures, they could accept squatter sovereignty and permit the people of any territory to decide whether the territory should be free or slave, or they could approve extension of the Missouri Compromise line to the Pacific.

No choice had been made as the country headed into the election of 1848. Moreover, both the Democrats and the Whigs were divided over the slavery issue. Both parties had many adherents in each section and both feared the consequences of a definite stand on either side of this vital question. In addition, many sincere men in both sections hoped above all to avoid the dissolution of the Union. The net result was that in 1848 both parties entirely ignored the slavery issue. Democratic nominee Lewis Cass ran upon a platform which made no mention of slavery; for General Zachary Taylor the Whigs provided no platform at all.

Clearly, here was opportunity for a third party. While some men of the old Liberty Party hoped to rally all antislavery forces behind the Wilmot Proviso, shrewder minds saw greater possibility for an antislavery ticket in a combination of abolitionists with the Barnburners of the Van Buren branch of the Democratic party. Working on this belief, the political abolitionists on August 9, 1848, called the opponents of slavery to a convention in Buffalo. There they adopted resolutions which proclaimed that territories must be kept free for "the hardy pioneers of our own land, and the oppressed and banished of other lands," and adopted the slogan, "Free Soil, Free Speech, Free Labor and Free Men." With a moderate antislavery man, Martin Van Buren, for President and Charles Francis Adams for Vice-President, the new Free-Soil Party had a ticket acceptable to antislavery men of every degree of feeling against the institution. The party polled three hundred thousand votes and again drew enough New York state ballots to give that state, and the election, to Taylor. The election of thirteen Free-Soilers to the House of Representatives and of extreme antislavery man Salmon P. Chase of Ohio to join New Hampshire's equally radical John P. Hale in the Senate indicated that politicians could not much longer avoid directly facing the slavery question. The new party had demonstrated the potential threat of political abolitionism.

So after Torrey's death the crusade against slavery went on in other areas. Moreover, the Mexican War, which the abolitionists saw as the slaveholders' bid for more territory, diverted attention to the political issues involved in the extinction of slavery. Nor did the thirty-first Congress which assembled in December, 1849, choose to avoid the slavery question. Early in the new year, Kentucky's Henry Clay presented to the Senate his compromise solution for the entire matter of organization and disposal of slavery in the Mexican cession. Of the five separate statutes which finally became the Compromise of 1850, the most disturbing to abolitionists was the new Fugitive Slave Act which severely punished those who aided slaves to escape, required federal officers to make extreme efforts to capture fugitives, denied a captured Negro the right to trial by jury, returned him to slavery upon a mere affidavit of a master or a master's agent, provided a five-dollar fee for a commissioner who turned a fugitive free but doubled the amount if he gave him over to the claimant. By 1850, then, abolitionists relied upon legalistic and political argument rather than upon the moral appeal. If they found that some Americans had difficulty seeing a relationship between the Mexican War and the ambitions of the slaveholders, they found the relationship becoming more apparent when the Compromise of 1850 occasioned debate amongst the country's most prominent political leaders. The martyrs after 1850 were those valiant souls who struggled against an iniquitous law.

Meanwhile, political abolitionists continued their efforts in politics. But the first years of the new decade showed little promise for them, as the Free-Soil Party's candidate, John P. Hale, polled only half as many votes in the 1852 election against Democrat Franklin Pierce and Whig General Winfield Scott as the party had gathered four years before. Indeed, by this time many in both North and South assumed that the Compromise of 1850 had permanently settled the slavery question. But this was far from true, for some Southerners were still demanding expansion, particularly into Cuba, and in addition, Northern opposition to the Fugitive Slave Act increased with every day. Then in 1854 Stephen A. Douglas sponsored the Kansas-Nebraska bill which applied the squatter sovereignty principle to two new western territories. The debates on the Kansas-Nebraska bill renewed all the animosity of the slavery discussions of the two previous decades and created chaos within the major political parties. Southerners of all parties backed the bill, Northern Democrats split over it, and the Whigs divided strictly along sectional lines. The year 1854, then, marked the passing of the "finality" of the Compromise of 1850.

Moreover, two other events of 1854 increased tension between the two sections and pointed up the injustice of the new fugitive slave law. In May of that year, Anthony Burns, Virginia-born literate slave-preacher, left the Richmond labors for which his master received payment and escaped to Boston. On May 24 officers there arrested him on a charge of theft and jailed him in an upper room of the courthouse. Two days later, when the town was full of conventioning abolitionists and women suffragists, as well as the curious from the whole countryside, Wendell Phillips, Theodore Parker, and Thomas W. Higginson urged Bostonians who attended a Faneuil Hall meeting to oppose compliance with the 1850 law. Amidst excitement which some likened to that of Revolutionary days in Boston, the town

Vigilance Committee rescued Burns by killing a United States marshal and battering down the door of the prisoner's room. Nevertheless, when Burns's master arrived, the United States commissioner readily accepted his identification and ordered the fugitive returned to Virginia. On June 2 a sullen crowd lined the curbs as Anthony Burns departed down State Street between the files of armed troops which President Franklin Pierce and the mayor of Boston had ordered to make certain his embarkation. Abolition journalists and lecturers told and retold the story and protested the wickedness of a law which remanded a man of Burns's caliber to chattel slavery. Within a few months abolitionists further demonstrated their opposition to the law by purchasing Burns and returning him North a free man.[1]

Also in 1854, a United States marshal in Wisconsin arrested a runaway Negro named Glover. When the Negro went to jail in Milwaukee, Sherman Booth, abolitionist editor of the *Free Democrat* published in that city, urged the people to insist upon a trial to determine Glover's status so that he would not be peremptorily returned to slavery. When the judge who jailed the Negro refused to honor a writ of habeas corpus for him, a mob freed the prisoner and helped him escape to Canada. In March federal officers sent Sherman Booth to the Milwaukee jail for his part in the Glover case. For the next few years Booth was in and out of both court and jail numerous times. In 1860, after a second hearing in a United States court, Booth became a federal prisoner in the Milwaukee customhouse. On August 1 of that year citizens rescued him and he fled the town. But in October federal authorities again arrested him in Berlin, Wisconsin, and returned him to jail in Milwaukee. There he remained until March 2, 1861, when President James Buchanan remitted his fine.[2]

Both the Burns case and the Booth case occasioned legalistic and political arguments of significance in the abolitionists' new area of opposition to slavery, for in the decade preceding the Civil War they returned to the doctrines of the rights-of-man philosophers and demanded for the Negro the same rights and privileges which the Constitution promised the white man. The greatest of these, so long as the fugitive slave law of 1850 remained on the books, was trial by jury for black men threatened with remand to involuntary servitude. In Boston, abolitionists raged that only his master's word was necessary to send Anthony Burns into slavery. In Milwaukee, Sherman Booth's counsel, attorney Byron Paine, contended that its provision for reduction to slavery without a jury trial made the fugitive slave law unconstitutional. Such legalistic and political arguments carried abolitionists a long way from their old insistence upon the sinfulness of a man's holding another in bondage. So, with the new arguments against slavery in the prewar decade, abolitionists turned also to legalistic and political weapons to fight the institution.

Chief among these were the personal liberty laws which a number of states adopted. In direct defiance of the hated federal statute, these laws in general forbade state officers to use state jails or prisons for holding fugitives, stiffened requirements for identification and proof of ownership, imposed heavy penalties for perjury and illegal seizures, and demanded jury trials to establish cause for returning a Negro to slavery. Such regulations, while greatly increasing the Southerner's difficulties in reclaiming his slaves, were at the same time even more potent in engendering bitterness and ill feeling between the two sections.

Meanwhile, men North and South moved to turn the Kansas-Nebraska bill to the advantage of their respective creeds. Although antislavery settlers moved into Nebraska without contest, such was not the case with Kansas. Fearing that Missourians would move there as surely as Iowans had into Nebraska, northern abolitionists organized to aid free-soil adherents to the new territory. The result for Kansas was the bloody clash of the proponents and opponents of slavery extension. Moreover, the Kansas troubles gave impetus to the political phase of the abolition movement. Even before the passage of the bill, the political abolitionists had started to redeem their venture from the position into which their inexperience, rather than popular disapproval of their doctrines, had placed the free-soil movement.

Early in 1854 opponents of the Kansas-Nebraska bill had met at Ripon, Wisconsin and resolved to organize as "Republicans." In July, Michigan citizens joined them with a statewide Republican organization. Shortly antislavery men in other states—Indiana, Ohio, Illinois, Iowa, New York, Vermont—followed. By fall of 1854 the new party was strong enough to defeat the Democrats in some midwestern states, to threaten them seriously in others, and in addition to show promise in parts of New England. During the following year leading antislavery Whig William H. Seward came over to the new party, and after him came individuals and groups with differing beliefs on numerous national and local questions other than slavery. Hence in 1856 the Republican party presented a platform which took a definite stand on only two issues: the abolition of slavery and of polygamy in United States territories. The party had no unified national campaign that year but in the various states it fought the Democrats on local issues. Thereafter the Republicans built state organizations through compromises which held the several factions together. Their 1860 platform included separate planks to satisfy the many groups, and called for a halt to the advance of slavery into the West. With this situation, the party managed, through state organizations and with the help of the split in the Democratic party, to elect Abraham Lincoln President. After twenty years the political abolitionists had achieved the political position which they had originally declared was necessary to the abolition of slavery.

Events of the decade since 1850, however, had furthered the return of abolitionism to the realm of a moral crusade. In 1852 Harriet Beecher Stowe published *Uncle Tom's Cabin* and Northerners raged at the injustice of the system she described. Then in 1857 the Supreme Court's decision in the Dred Scott case convinced many that the legalistic and political approach to abolition could lead to solutions based not upon the application of broad general principles but upon the attitudes of the men in power at a given time. But, above all, the struggle which ensued as both free- and slave-state men raced their proponents into Kansas disheartened even abolitionists on the efficacy of the legalistic and political approach to the destruction of slavery. The situation in "bleeding Kansas" was no testimonial for the squatter sovereignty principle. Yet out of the Kansas struggle came the means of returning the abolition crusade to its moral basis.

He
Being Dead
Yet
Speaketh

CHARLES T. Torrey's death rounded out an impressive list of abolition martyrs. The movement which had begun with the faint protests of a few Puritans and Quakers, developed with the organization of scattered societies, and quickened with the prophetic vehemence of William Lloyd Garrison's pen, had before mid-century become a fiery crusade whose zealots displayed all the characteristics of the Christian martyrs. Abolition journalists and lecturers could review the names of those who had sacrificed for the cause of the slave: Prudence Crandall, Theodore Weld, James G. Birney, James E. Burr, Alanson Work, George Thompson, Jonathan Walker, Stephen S. Foster, Parker Pillsbury, Henry B. Stanton, and the rest of the evangelizing Seventy. The sacrifice of two men who had died for the cause glorified the entire list and the whole movement. Jesus had said, "Greater love hath no man than this, that a man lay down his life for his friends." Elijah Parish Lovejoy and Charles Turner

Torrey had demonstrated the great love of the American abolitionist for his colored brethren. But in the decade after Torrey's sacrifice, abolitionists turned from moral to legalistic and
political arguments against slavery. The crusade came back to
its old appeal only when another man laid down his life for the
slave. The new martyr, merging humanitarianism with political
abolitionism, became a sacrifice to a new antislavery synthesis.

Born at Torrington, Connecticut, in 1800, John Brown spent
his childhood there and in the Western Reserve at Hudson,
Ohio. From his father he learned the tanner's trade and in the
woods near his home he learned to use a gun. His interest in
school, he admitted, extended only to opportunities for play,
for wrestling, and for childish pranks. Subject to spells of melan-
choly, young John Brown suffered long and intensely over such
childhood tragedies as the disappearance of a pet squirrel, the
death of a pet lamb, and the loss of a favorite marble which an
Indian friend had given him. When he was eight, his mother
died, and he mourned through a prolonged period of incon-
solable grief.

But Brown himself thought another tendency his greatest
childhood problem. "I must not neglect to tell you of a very
bad & foolish habbit to which John was somewhat addicted,"
he wrote in his autobiography to a young friend. "I mean *tell-
ing lies:* generally to screen himself from blame; or from punishment."[1]

By the time he was twenty, John Brown had gone east to
prepare for the ministry, given up the career because eye trouble interfered with his study, returned to Hudson to set up his
own tanning business and to take his younger brother to live
with him in the cabin which he built for himself, hired a house-
keeper, and married the woman's daughter. From her marriage
in 1820 until her death in childbirth in 1832, Dianthe Lusk
Brown did her housework to the accompaniment of her own
loud psalm singing, Scripture reading, and the prattling of some
of the seven children to whom she gave birth in twelve years.
The year following her death John Brown, then thirty-three,

married sixteen-year-old Mary Ann Day. Of their thirteen children, seven died in childhood, four of them in less than three weeks of 1842. When Brown went into bankruptcy shortly thereafter, the court permitted him to keep all of his eleven Bibles, his copy of "Beauties of the Bible," and "Church Members' Guide," along with a few farm animals and three pocket knives.

At the age of twelve, John Brown later remembered, he came under conviction of the sin of slaveholding. Out of the haze of childhood memories, he recounted that when he was twelve he delivered some of his father's cattle some one hundred miles from home and at his destination spent the night with a family which owned a Negro boy about his own age. As the master showered attention and kindness upon him, Brown pondered the contrast between his free life and that of orphan slave children. He remembered that he wondered, "Is God their Father?"[2] It was after this experience, he recalled, that he, in the true tradition of abolition's self-anointed prophets, swore eternal war against American slavery. At sixteen he joined the Congregational church and began the study of the Bible with the same enthusiasm and energy which he applied to any physical task. In 1839 he announced to his family that he believed slavery could be destroyed only through a blood atonement.

Between 1825 and 1850 John Brown, forgetting for most of a quarter-century his youthful consecration, engaged in various businesses—tanning leather, sheep herding, wool selling. He traveled over a good part of the United States and even went to Europe to market wool. During this period he was defendant in twenty-one law suits brought to recover money lent him on promissory notes, for payments due wool growers whose product he had accepted for sale, for wages due employees, or for nonfulfillment of contracts. In all but four of the cases the decision was unfavorable to him. Not until 1849 did Brown have occasion to remember the vows of his youth. In that year he settled his family on a farm which was part of the large acreage which Gerrit Smith had set aside in his Adirondack property at North Elba in Essex County, New York, for the use

John Brown and his men taken in the engine house at Harper's Ferry. Illustrated papers were full of such sketches.

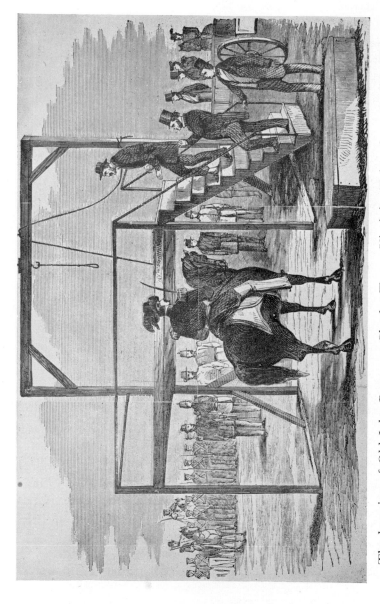

The hanging of Old John Brown at Charles Town, Virginia. Taken from *Leslie's Illustrated Newspaper* of December 17, 1859.

The Sixth Massachusetts Regiment fighting their way through Baltimore. They were "the first martyrs in the fratricidal battle."

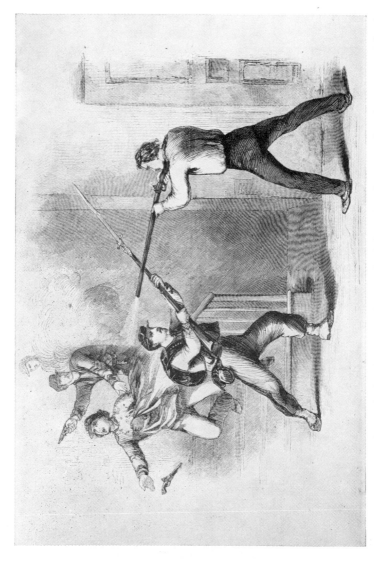

Colonel Elmer Ellsworth, having torn down Virginia's flag from an inn in Alexandria, is shot by a Southerner. In turn a Union soldier kills the Virginian.

of free Negroes. Brown promised not only to live amongst the freedmen there, but also offered to teach them how to clear the forests and ready their farms for production.

John Brown, who admitted a tendency to dictate to others, esteemed force. He studied the guerilla warfare of Spain and of the Caucasus; he knew all the movements of the freedmen of Haiti; he admired Napoleon and Napoleon's methods. Indeed, in 1849 when he went to Europe to market the wool which a number of American growers assigned to him, he spent so much time on a side visit to France to make a detailed study of Napoleon's battlefields that he completely neglected his business.

Slowly his military interests and his concern with enslaved Africans made a synthesis in his mind: Negroes might be made into soldiers! In the eighteen-forties John Brown dreamed of liberating Southern Negroes. He would combine the techniques of guerilla warfare with those of the Haitian freedmen and direct all with the skill of Napoleon. "My plan," he said, "is to take at first about twenty-five picked men, and begin on a small scale; supply them with arms and ammunition, and post them by squads of five on a line of twenty-five miles. The most persuasive of these shall go down to the fields from time to time, as opportunity offers, and induce the slaves to join them, seeking and selecting the restless and daring."[3] In 1850 be banded together the free Negroes of Springfield, Ohio, into the League of the Gileadites. They must learn, he told them, to resist slave catchers. "Nothing," he said, "so charms the American people as personal bravery. . . . Think of the number who have been mobbed and imprisoned on your account! Have any of you seen the Branded Hand? Do you remember the names of Lovejoy and Torrey? . . . Should one of your number be arrested, you must collect together as quickly as possible so as to outnumber your adversaries. . . . Let no ablebodied man appear on the ground unequipped or with his weapons exposed to view. . . . By going about your business quietly you will get the job disposed of before the number that an uproar would bring together can collect."[4] John Brown would give the Negro weapons, and then, with Napoleonic genius, lead him out of bondage.

In the spring of 1855 John Brown's sons went to Kansas. There they joined the "Free Staters" and wrote to their father at the farm in New York. John junior wanted guns for the frontier struggle and the father set about to collect Sharpe's rifles and money to purchase all kinds of arms. New England abolitionists and antislavery men in other parts of the country where John Brown was known readily contributed. At a convention in western New York, Brown told how four of his sons were already fighting the free-state battle in Kansas and added that three more would go if they could but finance the journey. Here, he said, was opportunity for abolitionists to do something practical for freedom, for "without the shedding of blood there is no remission of sin."[5] Indeed, he promised that if money and guns were available, he himself would go west with his three remaining sons. Next day Gerrit Smith[6] came before the meeting to present Brown with a musket and bayonet, a voltaic repeating pistol and a short broadsword for each of his seven sons. Gratefully John Brown accepted the weapons and the sixty dollars collected from the conventioners. At other similar meetings he accepted additional money and arms for the Kansas struggle. In September, 1855, he followed his sons west.

From this time until his death on the scaffold four years later, John Brown was terror to proslavery men in his adopted territory. In 1855 in the War on the Wakarusa he headed the "Liberty Guards" and at the conclusion of the fighting he made an abolition speech in which he suggested that the proper way to settle the free-or-slave-state issue was to arm men with guns and bayonets and make night raids on the camps of the Southern "border ruffians."

On the night of May 25, 1856, armed men called from their beds five alleged proslavery men who lived along the Pottawatomie Creek in Kansas and murdered them in cold blood. The plan of attack and the method of killing and butchering followed Brown's recommendations for such work. Although John junior went to jail for three months for suspected complicity, the father eluded both local and federal troops and returned to his cabin on Osawatomie Creek.

During the summer of 1856 abolitionists feverishly collected rifles and ammunition for the free-state cause in Kansas. The Kansas Committee of Massachusetts, with George L. Stearns as chairman, and Franklin Sanborn, Thomas W. Higginson, Theodore Parker, and Dr. Samuel G. Howe as members, raised money to equip free-staters with Sharpe's rifles and made John Brown their agent for receiving the equipment. Seventy-nine "rifle Christians" left the East, with a special blessing from Henry Ward Beecher: "We will not forget you. Every morning breeze shall catch the blessings of our morning prayers and roll them westward to your prairie home."[7]

In August, Brown organized an "army" for the defense of the Osawatomie settlement. Shortly this group engaged in battle with proslavery men at Sugar Creek. When it was over, John Brown appeared in the settlement, as was his custom after such encounters, driving before him one-hundred and fifty head of liberated cattle and a dozen or more horses. After the death of his son Frederick in a skirmish with "slave staters" he decided that the place to attack the slave system was right in the Southern states. John Brown determined to carry the war into "Africa." Moreover, when September brought John junior's release from jail, the father sent the young martyr's chains to Henry Ward Beecher who exhibited them in Brooklyn's Plymouth Church to encourage contributions for the Kansas cause. In March when Brown journeyed to his Adirondack farm— where he subsequently stayed only two weeks because he could not ignore, as he said, the "sobbing of the slaves" which was ever in his ear as he tried to sleep—he took the chains and exhibited them when he spoke in the town hall in Concord, Massachusetts.

From North Elba, Brown went to Collinsville, Connecticut,

solicited money, and ordered a thousand six-foot pikes from a local blacksmith. Then he proceeded to New York to arrange for the training of his projected army of "volunteer regulars." By late summer, 1857, John Brown and his personal followers were gathered at Tabor, Iowa. There they stored Kansas-bound rifles and munitions which abolitionists entrusted to Brown; there they met for military instruction and for planning their strategy for the "invasion of Africa."

In 1858 John Brown proceeded to the details of his plan to carry the war to Southern doorsteps. Early that year he conferred with several Eastern abolitionists, indicated that he would soon be ready to make the big move, sent John junior to look over the area and people around Harper's Ferry, Virginia, and prepared to accept additional funds which his backers were still collecting. On April 29 he and nine others slipped into Chatham, Ontario, on Lake Erie and spent ten days setting up a "Provisional Constitution and Ordinance for the People of the United States." This document, after declaring slavery a war of one portion of citizens against another, called for the establishment of a constitution which would enable "citizens of the United States, and oppressed peoples," better to protect their "Persons, Property, Lives and Liberties." It invited all persons of mature age to its banner and outlined a confused imitation of the American Constitution. To the important post of Commander in Chief of the army, the conferees elected John Brown. His job was to "direct all movements of the army, and advise with any allies." Others present were to become president, vice-president, treasurer, secretary of state, secretary of war, secretary of the treasury, and judges under the new regime.[8] The move into Africa was near.

From Canada John Brown returned to Kansas, this time disguised as one "Shubal Morgan." Without funds, he tried to borrow money from the Kansas National Committee agent in Lawrence. Then late in the year he made a foray into Missouri and returned with eleven Negroes, ten horses, three yoke of oxen, eleven mules, and a quantity of bedding, clothing, and provisions. The slaves John Brown conducted to Canada; the goods he sold. Slave-keepers had no property rights which freedom lovers were bound to respect.

In January, 1859, John Brown left Kansas, for he said his work there was done. On his way east he accepted Congressman Joshua Giddings' invitation to speak in the church at Jefferson, Ohio. He addressed other meetings in the town halls in Peterboro, New York, and in Concord. In Boston he visited members of the Kansas Committee, and received money. Before he left New England for the Harper's Ferry region he ordered another five hundred dollars worth of pikes.

In July, 1859, John Brown rented a farm five miles from Harper's Ferry, set October for his "invasion of Africa," and trimmed down his long white beard. On the fifteenth of that month he sent his six uninitiated men to the farmhouse attic to hear another colleague read the constitution of the Provisional Government. Then the Commander in Chief himself went up and administered the oath of fidelity and secrecy. At eight o'clock that night he assembled his army and started down the mountain for the town of Harper's Ferry.

With them John Brown arrived after midnight—Monday, for he would not defile the Sabbath—and Brown posted guards along the bridge over the Shenandoah, seized the United States arsenal buildings, and made prisoners of the street loafers who happened along. Then with three others he marched half a mile up the river and captured the rifle shops. He then controlled the strategic points at Harper's Ferry. But Brown yearned for one more conquest. He had heard that one Colonel Lewis Washington, a resident of the vicinity, owned the sword of Frederick the Great and the pistols of LaFayette. So he assigned men to capture the colonel and designated one Negro to bring him the sword, and another to deliver the guns. When they carried out the order, they made the white man walk and permitted his slaves to ride.

Brown gave pikes to the few Negroes who straggled in from nearby farms and visioned the legions of others he would liberate and arm as he proceeded through the Southern states bringing the war into Africa. Before the outside world heard of the events at Harper's Ferry, the raiders took one life, that of a free Negro whom they accidentally killed as he went about his work as the railroad baggage master at Harper's Ferry.

Alarms quickly went out in all directions and by daylight militiamen arrived. Brown and his army barricaded themselves in the engine house attached to the arsenal. But they had set their own trap, for by noon the town was full of soldiers. At intervals during the rest of the day, John Brown, wearing the Frederick the Great sword, would open the engine-house door a crack and solemnly listen to requests that he surrender. But the parleys came to nothing because Brown refused to give up unless he could remove his prisoners, supplies, and all of his own men, dead or alive, to the Maryland hills. When, on Tuesday morning, October 18, he suggested such terms to Robert E. Lee's emissary, J. E. B. Stuart, the marines used sledge hammers and then a ladder as a battering ram to break down the door. Once inside, a lieutenant dashed at Brown to bayonet him, missed, then beat him to unconsciousness. Brown's prisoners filed out and Lee conducted the revived Brown to the office of the army paymaster for questioning. But to all queries he answered that he had meant no harm, but only wanted to liberate slaves. He was but a tool of Providence, and God had sent him to Harper's Ferry. John Brown went to jail in Charles Town, Virginia.

Just one week after his capture Brown stood trial in the Jefferson County courthouse. A jury indicted him and four of his six men who were still alive, on three counts: treason to the state of Virginia, conspiracy with Negroes to commit treason, and murder in the first degree.

John Brown came into court on a stretcher and ignored the entire proceedings of his dramatic and much publicized trial, except for a brief moment when he sat bolt upright to protest a witness's reference to instances of insanity in his family as a reason for leniency for him. When the court gave him a chance to speak for himself, his address drew him praise from abolitionists and other sympathizers all over the land.

"If you seek my blood," he said, "you can have it at any moment, without this mockery of a trial. I have had no counsel. I have not been able to advise with anyone. I know nothing about the feelings of my fellow-prisoners, and am utterly unable to attend in any way to my own defence. My memory don't serve me. My health is insufficient, although improving. There are mitigating circumstances that I would urge in our favor, if a fair trial is to be allowed us. But if we are to be forced with a mere form—a trial for execution—you might spare yourselves that trouble. I am ready for my fate. I do not ask a trial. I beg for no mockery of a trial—no insult—nothing but that which conscience gives, or cowardice would drive you to practise. I ask again to be excused from the mockery of a trial. I do not even know what the special design of this examination is. I do not know what is to be the benefit of it to the Commonwealth. I have now little further to ask, other than that I may not be foolishly insulted only as cowardly barbarians insult those who fall into their power."[9] The Virginia court heard him in patience, then on November 2 passed sentence.

John Brown would hang at Charles Town on December 2, 1859, and the sovereign state of Virginia made ready his gallows. Even as the New York *Journal of Commerce* said editorially that hanging would immortalize him but imprisonment would commit him to oblivion, the scaffold builders hammered away in a cornfield outside the town.[10] At Virginia Military Institute Thomas Jonathan Jackson's cadets shouldered their packs and left for Charles Town; Robert E. Lee returned his marine unit, re-enforced by United States artillerymen, to Harper's Ferry to protect the vicinity until after the execution. Governor Henry Wise would not gamble on the falsity of the reports he heard of abolitionist bands preparing to swoop down to rescue "Old Brown." Baltimore and Ohio Railroad officials barred from their December first and second runs east of Wheeling all passengers except those who could present a written character reference from a station agent.

On November 30 Governor Wise provided a carriage for Mrs. John Brown to go from Harper's Ferry to see her husband. The big, rawboned woman listened to his final advice and instructions for handling the affairs of the family for whom she had for so long shouldered the responsibility, first while Brown traveled about his business interests and, recently, while he used the "sword" which he believed God had put in his hand. After a last meal together, Mary Brown solemnly parted from her husband and went back to wait in Charles Town to claim his body.

Sometime before eleven on the morning of December 2, the jailer came for Old John Brown. He went with steady gait out to the wagon which was to take him to the place of execution. Two guards took their places on either side of the vehicle. Old John Brown climbed in and settled himself on the seat provided for him—atop his own coffin. The three companies of infantry ahead began to move. Other foot soldiers fell in beside the wagon. Behind them the mounted troops gently spurred their horses. John Brown moved to his execution. At the foot of the steps to the scaffold he rose and jumped lightly, unaided, from the wagon. Soldiers methodically lifted his coffin and placed it beside the gallows. Old John Brown mounted the steps quickly and with steady tread. He stood without flinching while soldiers attended to final arrangements. For twelve long minutes he waited on the trap door while the large military escort deployed in the cornfield. Then there were a few seconds of silence, the trap door opened, and Virginia had her vengeance and abolition had a new martyr.

In the following days Americans faced the full force of what this new and dramatic martyrdom would mean to the deepening rift between North and South. Northern newspapers, individual abolitionists, writers, and ministers of the Gospel, expressed themselves frequently and forcefully. Indeed, just six days after the verdict, Ralph Waldo Emerson bespoke the attitude of many when he lectured in Boston on "Courage." He reviewed the stories of early martyrs, then concluded: "Look nearer, at the ungathered records of those who have gone to languish in prison or to die in rescuing others, or in rescuing themselves from chains of the slave: or look at that new saint, than whom none purer or more brave was ever led by love of man into conflict and death; a new saint, waiting yet his martyrdom; and who, if he shall suffer, will make the gallows glorious like the cross."[11]

The speed with which Virginia hanged Brown, said the *New York Tribune,* might well make a martyr of him. "So let us be reverently grateful for the privilege of living in a world rendered noble by the daring of heroes, the suffering of martyrs— among whom let none doubt that History will accord an honored niche to old John Brown." The New York *Independent* concluded its review of Brown's execution with, "The hero and leader of that desperate and daring enterprise has suffered the full sentence of the law, but suffered it in such a way as to turn its ignominy into honor, and its penalty into martyrdom." Editorially the same paper commented that although John Brown the traitor and outlaw lived no more, John Brown the prophet and friend of the oppressed survived, "a power greater than the state that condemned him, and the army that encompassed his scaffold." The Boston *Christian Register* called him a fanatic and declared reason our only safety, but feared his death did not end his influence. In Chicago the *Christian Times and Illinois Baptist* said everyone made too much of the story and Governor Wise's actions were ridiculous. Indeed, the *Times* concluded, politicians should stop capitalizing on the event and the country would quiet down.[12] The Lawrence, Kansas, *Republican* wailed that his trial was unfair and his treatment inexcusable. The New York *Observer* called Brown a "fanatical abolitionist" whose crimes should not be tolerated, at the same time that the Syracuse *Wesleyan* called him a martyr and one of the bravest men who ever lived.[13] William Lloyd

Garrison, true to his nonviolence principles, could not approve Brown's use of weapons. Hence the *Liberator* confined itself to reporting all proceedings with little editorial comment, publication of attitudes from other editors, and communications and poems of praise sent in by readers. Garrison did say once, however, after calling Brown's scheme misguided, wild, and apparently insane, ". . . but let no one who glories in the revolutionary struggle of 1776 deny the right of the slaves to imitate the example of our fathers."[14]

Avowed abolitionists hailed Brown as another martyr to their cause. On November 1 Wendell Phillips spoke on "Lessons of the Hour" at Brooklyn Plymouth Church. He quoted Lydia Maria Child's letter in which she had told Governor Wise that Brown was a saint:

> Right forever on the scaffold,
> Wrong forever on the throne;
> But that scaffold sways the future
> And behind the dim unknown
> Standeth God within the shadow
> Keeping watch above his own.

In mid-December Phillips spoke again, this time before the Twenty-eighth Congregational Society of Theodore Parker in Music Hall in Boston. He referred to the glorious martyrdom of the hero-saint and concluded, "John Brown is the impersonation of God's order and God's law, moulding a better future, and setting for it an example."[15] At the same time the *National Anti-Slavery Standard* said editorially, "And the few who in our time, recognize and declare the essential resemblance in character between Jesus, the crucified, and that modern man, sent from God, whose name was John—the few who say that 'the martyrdom of the latter, if it shall be perfected, will make the gallows glorious, like the cross'—are now accused of impiety and blasphemy by men whose strength is to sit still and whose piety is shown by praying that God should do their duty for them!"[16] Charles C. Burleigh told the annual meeting of the Massachusetts Anti-Slavery Society that Brown's power over men was due to his willingness to self-sacrifice.[17] John G. Whittier wrote a poem, "Brown of Osawatomie," which a number of newspapers published.[18] Ralph Waldo Emerson told a Brown Relief meeting in Salem, Massachusetts, that the Brown family came of some of New England's best stock. Henry D. Thoreau gave his lecture, "A Plea for Captain John Brown," at Concord and in Boston. He called Brown a common man and a Puritan who gave all to free Kansas. He called him a hero and an angel of light. "These men," he said, "in teaching us how to die, have at the same time taught us how to live," and concluded that he feared hearing that Brown might be spared, for his death would be more effective than his life.[19]

Ministers of various denominations prepared, and some published in pamphlet form, sermons in praise of John Brown. A New York Presbyterian used Bible texts to prove Brown and his followers completely right. Another said the community had been thrilled by news of his insurrection.[20] On Sunday evening, October 30, Henry Ward Beecher told an audience in Brooklyn's Plymouth Church, "Let no man pray that Brown be spared. Let Virginia make him a martyr."[21] The following week James Freeman Clarke, pastor of the Church of the Disciples in Boston and secretary of the American Unitarian Association, preached in Indiana Place Chapel in Boston from the text, "And Herod feared John, knowing that he was a just man." All those who believe slavery wrong, who justify the American Revolution, admire Washington and eulogize La-Fayette, he said, must believe Brown a hero and a martyr to principle.[22] On November 6, 1859, Gilbert Haven preached at the Harvard Street Methodist Episcopal Church in Cambridge on "The Beginning of the End of American Slavery." He said, in part, "He will make the scaffold in this land as sacred and potent as it became in England when Vane, and Sidney, and Russell mounted it." On November 27 Edwin M. Wheelock repeated in Boston Music Hall a sermon which he had originally preached in his church in Dover, New Hampshire, from the text, "And all men mused in their hearts of *John*, whether he

was the Christ or not." John Brown, he said, was the first plague
launched by Jehovah at the head of this immense and embodied
wickedness. "The Christ of anti-slavery has sent forth its 'John'
and forerunner. . . . The gallows from which he ascends into
heaven will be in our politics what the cross is in our religion. . . ." George Barrell Cheever called his address "The
Marytr's Death and the Martyr's Triumph" and said Brown's
trial was that of a true martyr. "John Fox's Book of Martyrs
being open before us, you might almost think a score of pages
had been taken from it to be rehearsed in Charlestown," he
said. He urged his audience to thank God that the first public
victim of the cruelty of slave-state law and despotism had been
a faithful servant of Christ.[23] On November 24 William H.
Furness said to an audience in the Unitarian Church in Philadelphia, "We cannot enter into that joy, we can hardly surmise
it, the joy of those who die, and who hold themselves the very
elect of God in that it is given them to die for a great and
beneficent principle. 'Blessed are ye,' said Jesus, 'who suffer
for Righteousness' sake. *Rejoice and be exceeding glad,* for
great is your reward in Heaven.' "[24] On December 4 the congregation of the Warren Street Methodist Episcopal Church in
Roxbury, Massachusetts, heard Fales Henry Newhall tell that
just as Jesus consecrated the cross, John Brown hallowed the
gibbet upon American soil. Out in Cincinnati a Congregational minister called Brown a martyr of noble faith, a God-
maddened old man.[25] Frederick Frothingham of Portland,
Maine, said Brown perished because he loved God with all his
heart and his neighbor as himself. Could there be, he asked, a
more suitable preparation for a thorough understanding of
the Master's death? "In Christ's death, sin was slain. In John
Brown's is slain the sin of slavery."[26]

In many parts of the country Brown's admirers and sympathizers gathered together to do him honor. Although most meetings occurred the day of his execution, some groups held them
earlier. On Saturday night, November 19, Bostonians met in

Tremont Temple to encourage aid to the family. Tickets sold for twenty-five cents and the committee also accepted additional contributions and urged the purchase of photographs, autographs, and copies of his address to the Virginia court. John A. Andrew, destined for the war governorship of the state, presided and read excerpts from recent Brown letters to abolitionists. John Brown, concluded Andrew, was a martyr to an idea. The Reverend J. M. Manning of Old South Church rose to say that God had "used this man as his sword." Ralph Waldo Emerson, who brought fifty dollars in collections for the martyr fund, referred to Brown as a Puritan who had reduced slavery to an absurdity. Wendell Phillips said Brown had achieved a martyrdom akin to that of the immortal Lovejoy and he had created needed publicity for the cause.[27]

On December 2 Tremont Temple welcomed another crowd to commemorate the execution of Old John Brown. Before the speaker's desk, against a black cross for background, stood a large photograph of Brown. Enclosing both cross and picture was a wreath of evergreen and amaranth. Large placards around the hall carried quotations from Brown, the Bible, Thomas Jefferson, and Patrick Henry. At the back of the stage stood a banner with the arms and seal of the sovereign state of Virginia. On the opposite side were placards bearing extracts from the constitution of that state—on equality. When the assigned time for the opening of the meeting came and the crowd settled down, a man went forward and raised near the platform a banner inscribed, "He dies by the mandate of the Slave Power, yet 'still lives' by virtue of his heroic deeds." Then Samuel May rose to announce the officers for the meeting and the program went along. Samuel E. Sewall, meeting chairman, said he had been sad all day for the martyred hero. Governor Wise he classed with Pontius Pilate; John Brown he placed beside William Tell, Robert Bruce, the Adamses, John Hancock, Joseph Warren, and George Washington. In similar vein, William Lloyd Garrison compared Brown with other Revolutionary heroes. Those who decry Brown do not love liberty, he said, and concluded, "Today, Virginia has murdered John Brown; tonight, we here witness his resurrection. . . .

> Onward, then, ye fearless band,
> Heart to heart, and hand to hand,
> Yours shall be the Christian's stand,
> Or the martyr's grave."[28]

At the services at Concord on the day of the execution, the Reverend E. H. Sears of Wayland prayed, "Let the blood of all thy martyrs for liberty, from ancient times down to this hour, cry to thee from the ground till the slave arises from his thralldom into the full glory of manhood." Thoreau told how the wife of a Boston judge visited John Brown in prison, mended for him his blood-stained clothes which he still wore, and then for a memento brought home a pin covered with his blood. A. Bronson Alcott read from Plato, Emerson read extracts from Brown's speeches and writings during his imprisonment. The meeting ended with the congregation singing a dirge.[29] On the same day the Negro congregation of the Twelfth Baptist Church started a meeting at the time of the scheduled execution at eleven in the morning and continued throughout the day with singing, praying, and speaking. Many colored people of Boston wore crepe or portraits of John Brown. In Harwich, Massachusetts, five hundred people heeded the tolling of the bells to enter Exchange Hall where the decorations included a gallows inscribed:

> John Brown—Friend of the Slave.
> Today, Virginia gives him a martyr's grave.[30]

On the day of the execution many Cleveland business houses closed as residents honored Brown in Melodeon Hall. A banner across the street on which the hall stood read, "I do not think I can better honor the cause I love than to die for it." Inside the building a large, gilt-framed photograph of John Brown hung over center stage and above it ran the motto, "Americus Humanis Generis," and to the left a banner reading, "John

Brown, the Hero of 1859." To the right another announced, "He being dead, yet speaketh." After Scripture reading and speeches the mourners solemnly filed out.[31]

At a meeting in the town hall in Northampton, Massachusetts, Charles C. Burleigh said the citizens of Virginia, rather than the man they had hanged, were criminal. Indeed, Burleigh was willing to forgive Brown for his use of force because the martyr was acting out his own faith. Another speaker displayed a framed original of a John Brown letter and the audience contributed to the martyr fund. In Clinton, Iowa, citizens responded to a circular from Samuel May and held two meetings, one to proclaim Brown a hero and the other to discuss the general problem posed by slavery in the United States. Towns in northern Illinois and southern Wisconsin arranged appropriate services—prayer meetings, lecture programs, the ringing of church bells, or the firing of cannon—and one Illinois citizen concluded that "John Brown has multiplied himself ten-thousandfold by his glorious death!" A meeting of the colored Anti-Slavery and Temperance Society of Worcester, Massachusetts, adopted resolutions calling the execution a blow to freedom, expressed sympathy for the family, and urged Negroes to purchase Brown's biography as a financial contribution to the family.

In Milford, Massachusetts, the ladies of James T. Woodbury's church made a door-to-door canvass and brought in one hundred dollars for the martyr fund. At Brookfield, Vermont, speakers reminded an audience that the "blood of the martyrs is the seed of the church" and concluded that John Brown's death would be avenged. The Cape Cod Anti-Slavery Society declared Brown a man almost unequalled in history.[32] On execution day Philadelphians heard William H. Furness, Lucretia Mott, and Mary Grew in National Hall. Albany residents had a choice of times for attending meetings, for the committee there planned three—at the hour of execution, in the afternoon, and in the evening—all preceded by a salute of one-hundred minute guns. On December 2 George B. Cheever conducted eleven o'clock services in New York's Church of the Puritans and Lewis Tappan led in prayer. Parker Pillsbury and Abram Pryne spoke to a meeting in Corinthian Hall in Rochester, New York. In Detroit the congregation of the Negro Second Baptist Church held an evening rally. Frederick Brown told a Cleveland audience of his brother's life and his hostility to slavery.[33] Out in Lawrence, Kansas, antislavery men met and condemned the institution, affirmed confidence in Brown and his actions, declared the right of the slave to protect himself from the tyranny of a master, then heard William A. Phillips praise Brown and conclude, "The time is coming, when an impartial posterity will calmly review the career of John Brown, —the cause for which he died,—and the men who remorselessly took his life; and looking from this generation to his sacrifice, will recognize in them the AGE and the MAN."[34] Ravenna, Ohio, residents rallied all who hate oppression and who sympathize with the devoted martyrs of liberty.[35] Dozens of other towns throughout the country scheduled meetings or brief acknowledgments of the execution hour. Among them were Marlboro, Haverhill, Abington, Natick, Milford, Fitchburg, Plymouth, New Bedford, Florence, all in Massachusetts; Birmingham, Connecticut; Syracuse, New York; and Waukegan, Illinois.[36] Towns along the route which the body followed to its burial at North Elba tolled church bells as the train passed through. At Elizabethtown, New York, where Mrs. Brown had to stay over a night, the body had an all-night guard of honor at the courthouse.

With so many familiar with the John Brown story, it achieved a commercial value. Before the end of the year the Baltimore and Ohio Railroad had to forbid sale of bogus "John Brown pikes" which an enterprising manufacturer sold on passenger trains in the Harper's Ferry area. Within a month after the execution three slavery plays were playing to New York audiences. Individuals advertised portraits of Brown and others connected with his trial.[37] The *Liberator* announced that one E. A. Brackett had completed a bust of him. One man advertised sale of portraits but said the profits would go to the family. Someone offered a card containing a picture, his autograph, and his replies to questions, all for fifteen cents or ten dollars for a hundred.[38] A publishing house announced a book which would be a compilation of letters of Brown sympathizers to him and his family, in addition to other interesting material.[39] Then in 1860 James Redpath, a newspaper correspondent who had witnessed some of the Kansas troubles and believed himself particularly equipped to present the John Brown story, published a volume. He dedicated his work to the Negro president of Haiti, General Fabre Geffrard, with, "But there are thousands in my country who have not yet bowed the knee to the Southern Baal. Preëminent among them was an heroic old man, who dared to defy the Slave Power in its oldest stronghold. He died for your race; he died for his country. He laid down his life to cover the foul stain on our national escutcheon, by endeavoring to liberate the bondmen of the Southern States."[40]

Redpath presented a variety of letters relating to John Brown, some written by relatives as he lay in the Charles Town jail, some from "Northern women," some from "Northern men," and some from "colored people." He included those which Lydia Maria Child and the wife of Senator James M. Mason of Virginia exchanged, statements of well-known people as to Brown's character and sincerity. He revealed to the public the singular requests which enthralled Americans made of John Brown—for a lock of his hair, for his autograph, for a message from the spirit world after his demise. He offered Victor Hugo's letter in praise of Brown, as well as some new poetry and some previously published in newspapers.

John Brown had become not only martyr, but legend. By the spring of 1861 some soldiers were singing a John Brown song to the tune of "Say, Brothers, Will you Meet Us?" In the latter part of May, the song sold as a penny ballad on Boston streets.[41] In 1863 Franklin Sanborn wrote a poem to John Brown, and Wendell Phillips read it at a ceremony at the Medford home of George L. Stearns who unveiled a marble bust of Brown in celebration of Emancipation Day, January 1.[42] In 1864 the *Liberator* advertised medallions of Brown at the same time that it announced that the families of the Harper's Ferry martyrs had received all the money from the martyr fund.[43] On August 31, 1882, Chicagoans held a reception for Mrs. Brown as she passed through the city on her way to Ohio to visit her children and on to her husband's grave at the old home at North Elba. She sat on the platform beside Elijah Lovejoy's sister and beneath a large picture of her husband which bore the inscription "Resistance to Tyrants is Obedience to God." She listened to the music of a band of colored soldiers, the remarks of a colored clergyman and to those of a white who called Brown God's ordained prophet and martyr. She acknowledged her introduction with a bow, but not one word. The audience sang "John Brown's Body" as they took leave of her.[44] On November 25, 1883, the *New York Tribune* published a Brown letter written in Charles Town jail a week before the execution. A month later the *Chicago Times* published professed eyewitness accounts of the murders in 1856 on the Pottawatomie. At Springfield, Massachusetts, the *Republican* bemoaned "partisan attacks" on Brown and threatened to get "true" statements from John Brown junior, and Franklin Sanborn. The fact that a statue of Brown might be one of two from Kansas to be set up in Washington occasioned these attacks, said the paper.[45] On May 8, 1884, Amos A. Lawrence presented portraits of John Brown and of Kansas Governor Charles Robinson, in addition to a file of Kansas newspapers, to the Massachusetts Historical Society. A short time later James Freeman Clarke told the same society that Brown was a Puritan of the old school who could not have had anything to do with the horrible murders on the Pottawatomie.[46] In late 1890 Franklin Sanborn published in *The Nation* a letter in which he explained that long before his martyrdom Brown had taken an oath to fight slavery to its finish.[47] In an article in 1916 on "Lovejoy's Influence on John Brown," one Justus N. Brown claimed that at a Lovejoy martyrdom meeting in November, 1837, John Brown had stood

up and said, "Here, before God, in the presence of these witnesses, from this time, I consecrate my life to the destruction
of slavery!"[48] So, said the author, John Brown could thank
Elijah Lovejoy for an insight into what do-or-die abolitionism
would mean and for an appreciation of a martyrdom for the
cause.

After more than a decade in which abolition arguments had
wandered into legalistic and political areas, Old John Brown
mounted the gallows in the sovereign state of Virginia and
faced his white compatriots. In him Northern men suddenly
saw a great humanitarian whose concern for the enslaved drove
him from home and family to defy the man-made laws of a slave
state in a daring expedition to break the chains of his black
brethren. Vicariously they suffered with him as he lay on his cot
in the court room, and as, pale and weak, he feebly rose for his
address to the court: "If you seek my blood, you can have it at
any moment. . . . I am ready for my fate." John Foxe had told
of no martyr of old who had spoken more sincerely or more self-
lessly. "Greater love hath no man than this, that a man lay down
his life for his friends," Jesus had said, and in the last days of
1859 John Brown's sacrifice brought back the Master's words to
many Americans. After the years of battling slavery with legalistic and political arguments, they again pondered the great love
of three men who had died for the Negro: Elijah P. Lovejoy,
Charles T. Torrey, and now John Brown. In the last, humanitarianism had merged with political abolitionism and he became a martyr to a new antislavery synthesis. Abolition had returned to the realm of a moral crusade. As such it was yet to
demand more sacrifices until even a greater leader should fall a
martyr to the struggle against the black man's bondage.

Who
Can Be
Against
Us?

JOHN Brown's death crystallized the attitudes of both South and North. He was bisymbolic. Southerners saw him as an embodiment of abolitionist, black Republican assault upon their constitutional rights. But Northerners saw him as a martyr to the great principles of freedom and liberty. He stood in the train of martyrs that ran back from Torrey through Henry B. Stanton, Parker Pillsbury, Stephen S. Foster, Jonathan Walker, George Thompson, Alanson Work, James E. Burr, James G. Birney, Theodore Weld, Prudence Crandall, and the immortal Elijah P. Lovejoy. He was an example of those who continued even until death for a great cause. John Brown's soul went marching on. With Abraham Lincoln's election Southerners steeled themselves against the extremes of abolitionist domination; every man of them would fight for freedom and liberty for the sovereign states of the South. With actual secession Northerners braced themselves to save the union. In both sections men would die for their cause.

Then, when on April 14, 1861, the news of Fort Sumter electrified the entire nation, the North suddenly saw itself on John Brown's scaffold, a victim of Southern tyranny. The South, decided the men of the free states, opposed the great principle of human liberty. Indeed, on April 15 when President Lincoln called for soldiers, a New York minister spoke the exalted view of millions of Northern men when he referred to conscience as a lamp to guide the wise, even though now and then it leads to martyrdom. "We had better," he concluded, "freely sacrifice our fortunes and our lives than allow the pestilent principles to prevail which have already struck disgrace upon our character. . . ."[1] Other patriots took up the call to martyrdom. The *Hartford Daily Courant* said editorially, "It is sweet to die for one's country; and never had mortal a better cause than that which now summons all who feel themselves to be men, to rally around the flag of our fathers."[2] In an editorial on "The Duties of the Hour" the New York *Independent* said Northerners should give full scope to the spirit of patriotic and Christian self-sacrifice for, "he who at such an hour as this draws back from the struggle or the sacrifice, is not worthy to be a man. What better thing can you do with your wealth than to spend it or to lose it in such a cause? What better thing can you do with your life than to lay it down in this conflict?"[3] Henry Ward Beecher told departing soldiers: "You go on a sacred mission. . . . And if you fall in that struggle, may some kind hand wrap around you the flag of your country, and may you die with its sacred touch upon you. It shall be sweet to go to rest lying in the folds of your country's banner, meaning, as it shall mean, 'Liberty *and* Union, now and forever!' "[4] The *Christian Register* took up the theme: "If this great patrimony of order and freedom, purchased by the blood of our fathers, seems to us too poor a thing to be kept by us at any cost—if we value it too little to feel that it is an honor and a privilege for us to be permitted to defend it, even at the cost of our lives and the lives of our children, then indeed there is no hope for us."[5] Said the *New York Tribune,* "Secession is to be crushed out in blood and fire if necessary," and Northerners agreed.[6] The martyr concept had political uses.

In Massachusetts Governor John A. Andrew was long since prepared for any contingency calling for military strength. He had endorsed the force techniques of the Kansas struggle and had hailed John Brown as a hero and a martyr. Since the day he took the oath of office he had been preparing for war and had urged readiness upon other New England states. Hence when Lincoln's call came Andrew already had regiments waiting and had only to assemble them. As the Sixth Massachusetts gathered before the capitol on April 17, Andrew told them the state had done everything in its power to prepare them for defense of Washington and for other national service. "We shall follow you with our benedictions, our benefactions, and prayers."[7] The first martyrs in the fratricidal battle were on their way.

On April 19 as the Sixth Regiment passed through Baltimore, they met resistance. Fighting their way across the city, they lost four of their number. Here was the first bloodshed of the war with four martyrs to freedom's crusade. Governor Andrew was as quick as ever an abolitionist organizer had been to seize upon them for the glory of his cause. "I pray you," he wired the mayor of Baltimore, "to cause the bodies of our Massachusetts soldiers, dead in Baltimore, to be immediately laid out, preserved with care, and tenderly sent forward by express to me. All expenses will be paid by this commonwealth."[8] On this message the *New York Times* commented, "Yes, bear the bodies 'tenderly'; they are more sacred than the relics of saints. Wherever they pass, let the Nation's flag, which they died to defend, wave over them; let cannon thunder the martial honor, and let women and children come to drop a tear over the Massachusetts dead, who died for Country and Liberty."[9] Four battered bodies in a Baltimore street symbolized all those who henceforth would lay down their lives for principles.

New martyrs came fast. A month after the Baltimore affair the Army of the Potomac moved into Alexandria, Virginia, on its premature advance upon Confederate soil. Among the officers of the first troops was Colonel Elmer E. Ellsworth, personal friend of President Lincoln and nationally known as commander of the Chicago National Guard Cadets. Before the war Ellsworth had toured the country with his unit, putting on exhibitions in weapon drill. The whole North felt a personal interest in him. Ellsworth entered Alexandria at the head of his regiment and faced the flag of the state of Virginia floating atop the Marshall House. He strode into the hotel, bounded up the stairs, and tore down the symbol of oppression and tyranny. But he had not reckoned with the zeal of the Virginians for their flag of freedom. As he prepared to leave the building with his souvenir, the proprietor fired a shot which sent Ellsworth sprawling, bloody and lifeless, into the folds of the flag of the Old Dominion. A fellow Union soldier, turned, fired, and the Southerner dropped. Though avenged, Ellsworth was another martyr.

The Northern public took its new martyr to its heart. Newspapers published large pictures of the noble hero of Alexandria in uniform and declared that he had died before the door of the very room in which George Washington had slept on a visit to the town. In New York City the Common Council met in special session and resolved that the colonel's martyrdom should encourage other men to enlist for the Union cause. In Ellsworth's funeral cortege Frank Brownell, slayer of the colonel's murderer, carried the bloody Virginia flag which the martyr had captured. Military officers announced that they would wear mourning badges for thirty days, and newspapers chronicled every detail of the Ellsworth story. *Leslie's Magazine* carried an extensive spread of scenes in Alexandria and added two sketches: a black-draped one of Ellsworth and another of his torn coat. Just three days after the shooting, photographer Mathew Brady advertised photographs of the hero, and within a week a publishing house announced that it would shortly

offer a military drill book identical with that used by the martyred friend of Abraham Lincoln. A stationer had Ellsworth
note paper and envelopes. A metalsmith offered medals inscribed on one side to "Ellsworth the Martyr" and on the other
to "Brownell the Avenger."

Other sufferers for the cause came rapidly, and each new
episode in the developing war was integrated into the martyr
concept. The religious martyrs had suffered imprisonment
from brutal jailers. So, too, had Prudence Crandall, James E.
Burr, Alanson Work, George Thompson, Jonathan Walker,
Stephen S. Foster, and Charles T. Torrey, the martyrs for
abolitionism. Some Northern men saw even the prisoners of
war as members of the martyr band. On July 21, 1861, the
Union forces suffered the humiliating defeat at Bull Run and
the Confederates suddenly had hundreds of prisoners—but no
prisons. Makeshift arrangements in and around Richmond
made for intolerable conditions, and within a few weeks Northerners seethed with anger at stories of atrocities in the Confederacy. Said the *New York Times* shortly after the battle:
"Most shocking stories begin to be reported of the barbarities
practised by the rebels upon the wounded men and prisoners
of the Union forces that fall into their hands. We are told of
their slashing the throats of some from ear to ear; of their
cutting off the heads of others, and kicking them about as foot-
balls; and of their setting up the wounded against trees, and
firing at them as targets, or torturing them with the plunges
of bayonets at their bodies. To cap the climax of atrocities, it
is stated that a hospital in which many wounded soldiers were
suffering extreme agony, or quietly yielding up the battle of
life, was fired upon and burned."[10] Another newspaper reported that an officer of a Massachusetts regiment heard a Confederate officer give the order to bayonet the men lying wounded
on the battlefield. Indeed, he said, they even trained their cannon on stretcher-bearers, fired on ambulances, and left buried
mines which exploded when Union soldiers moved into evacuated places and stepped on them. Concluded the paper, "We

are dealing with men who have little of the honor of civilized people. They show the temper and method of savages, and we should bear it in mind to avoid all the traps we can."[11] On May 23, 1862, George W. Julian told his colleagues in the House of Representatives, "They [the people] know that it [the South] gives arsenic to our soldiers, mocks at the agonies of wounded enemies, fires on defenceless women and children, plants torpedoes and infernal machines in its path, boils the dead bodies of our soldiers in cauldrons, so that it may make drinking cups of their skulls, spurs of their jaw bones and finger joints, as holiday presents for 'the first families of Virginia'. . . ."[12]

At the same time a fiery Tennesseean was capitalizing on his sufferings at the hands of the slaveholders. William G. "Parson" Brownlow, carpenter-minister-editor, had fought both states' rights and abolitionism. A supporter of slavery, but a staunch unionist as well, Brownlow thundered against Southern disunionists and, in November, 1860, declared that he would rebel against any Southern Confederacy. In 1861 he scattered pro-Union handbills all over East Tennessee and when his state seceded he filled the columns of his newspaper, the *Knoxville Whig*, with denunciations of the Confederacy. He professed to expect arrest any day, but the Confederate authorities ignored him and his editorials. Late in 1861 he announced to friends that for the safety of his family he would have to flee. He disappeared into the mountains of East Tennessee and then into the Great Smokies. But in a few weeks he returned to within six miles of Knoxville and began negotiations with the Confederate military authorities in charge there. Finally they granted him a passport out of the Confederacy. But when he got permission to stay an extra day, the civil authorities took that day to arrest him for high treason against the Confederate States. The Parson immediately sought aid from the military, but the officers ignored him and the civil authorities sent him to Knoxville jail. There he lectured to the prisoners, began an elaborate diary, proclaimed that the Southerners were going to hang him, and began composition of a speech to be made from the gallows. Early in March, 1862, Confederate Secretary of War Judah P. Benjamin ordered passports for Brownlow's exit through the Cumberland passes. On March 15 a buggy flying the white flag stopped within the Union lines some five miles out of Nashville. A tall, wiry man alighted quickly and eagerly rushed toward the federal soldiers. Parson Brownlow introduced himself and shook hands all around.

Here was a man who knew from experience the wickedness and barbarity of the Southerners, and Northerners could not hear enough of him. The soldiers escorted him to the best hotel in Nashville and the Parson began to broadcast his story. The jail in Knoxville, he told the crowd which gathered before the hotel, was a terrible place, and he had suffered much there. Indeed, the Parson did little more than elaborate on this theme —Southern barbarity and his martyrian sufferings therefrom— throughout the long tour which lasted from March until October and carried him through a large part of the North. Everywhere civic leaders assumed responsibility for the Parson's recognition and welfare; everywhere he repaid them with a superb show of anti-Southern pyrotechnics.

Through it all the Parson confirmed Northerners' fears of Southern character and savage practice. The spirit of secession, as they had suspected, was the spirit of murder, of assassination, in short, as the Parson put it, of hell. Confederate soldiers were not above cutting off the heads of their Yankee victims and displaying them out the windows of the cars as they went by train to another assignment. Indeed, at Greenville, Tennessee, said Brownlow, the rebels hung two Union men above the railroad tracks and ordered all engineers to take their trains slowly by so that passengers could strike them. At Knoxville they tied men to logs and rolled them along until their backs were cut to pieces. In other parts of Tennessee they administered beatings to women. The Parson was clearly no abolition martyr. Yet even he could fit into the tradition, as he had suffered as the martyrs had suffered from the tyranny of slaveholders. In addition, his sufferings gave point to his evidence of Southern cruelty and barbarity and in turn emphasized the martyrdom of the thousands of Union soldiers who endured torture or death for the Northern cause.

During the rest of the war the North read of Southern atrocities upon their brethren. In 1863 Percy Howard's pamphlet told of the arbitrary killing of contrabands and Union sympathizers, of inhuman treatment of wounded, of the deliberate burning of hospitals, and of unspeakable desecration of Union dead. Too, Southern women were as cruel as the men.

Then in 1864 Northerners saw in the report of the prison investigation committee of the United States Sanitary Commission confirmation of all the worst stories of conditions in Southern prisons. The testimony taken from returned prisoners revealed that even after three years of war, the housing conditions were no better than at the beginning. In Richmond there were no barracks, and sanitation arrangements bred disease. Cells beneath the prison where green slime covered the walls received those guilty of infringement of prison rules. Sometimes, for want of room in these crowded cells, men had to stand all night. In at least one prison, animals could come in from the street to feed upon coffinless bodies consigned there. Most prisoners lost any valuable possessions they had through robbery by their guards. The sick received no particular attention and guards amused themselves by wanton killing of prisoners.

Food conditions were even worse. Richmond prisoners complained of cob and husk in their coarse bread and of worms and maggots floating in the weekly pint of black peas. Prison officials or guards appropriated food and clothing parcels.

Belle Isle prison camp stood on a James River sand bar opposite Richmond. Although the far part of the island was densely wooded, the part comprising the camp was treeless, and the Confederates did not supply tents or houses. During the day the men endured the burning sun and at night slept on the ground, even in drenching rains. When prisoners came in, guards confiscated blankets and overcoats. Everything quickly became lice-infested. In cold weather men froze to death. Food complaints paralleled those in the Richmond prisons—musty bread, wormy soup, and tainted meat. Some prisoners testified that they had at times found provisions which the Confederates were simply refusing to issue. "The conclusion is inevitable," declared the committee report. "It was in their power to feed sufficiently, and to clothe, whenever necessary, their prisoners of war. They were perfectly able to include them in their military establishment; but they chose to exclude them from the position always assigned to such, and in no respect to treat them like men taken in honorable warfare." High point of the report was testimony concerning the condition of the bodies of those who died on Belle Isle: "No words can describe their appearance. In each case the sunken eye, the gaping mouth, the filthy skin, the clothes and head alive with vermin, the repelling bony contour, all conspired to lead to the conclusion that we were looking upon the victims of starvation, cruelty, and exposure, to a degree unparalleled in the history of humanity."[13] One edition of the report included pictures of emaciated victims who, by exchange or parole, barely escaped death from starvation. The same committee's reports on the excellent accommodations and provisions given Confederates in federal prisons confirmed the Northern attitude that Union soldiers were martyrs for righteousness and freedom.

Then came the news of Fort Pillow. This stronghold, situated on the Mississippi some eighty miles above Memphis, had been held by Union forces ever since the Confederates evacuated it in June, 1862. Two years later it was garrisoned by parts of the Second and Fourth colored United States Artillery. At daybreak on April 12, 1864, General Nathan Bedford Forrest's cavalry attacked Pillow with such force that the federals shortly withdrew behind its fortifications. At this Forrest closed in and gave the Unionists a half hour in which to surrender.

Reports of events after the surrender shocked and horrified the Northern public. Foxe's *Book of Martyrs* told no more terrible tales than did the congressional committee which reported on the Fort Pillow massacre. The Southerners, said the official document, entered the fort under flag of truce and murdered the surrendering garrison. They butchered the sick and wounded and set fire to the hospital. One Negro told of seeing a white man burned to ashes after he had been nailed through the hands and feet to the side of a house. Another said the rebels fastened a Union soldier by the clothing to a tent floor and then fired the tent. Others said they saw Northern soldiers buried alive and that on the morning after the surrender the Southerners went out on the battlefield and killed the wounded left there.

Leslie's Magazine declared: "A MASSACRE, savage in conception, savage in execution, and savage in its cold endorsement by the rebels at the South and their minions at the North, has horrified the land."[14] The Northern public read and mourned its martyrs to liberty.

Poetry and songs of the war as well emphasized the martyr concept. Shortly after Lincoln's call for troops, recruits marched off singing "We Are Coming, Father Abraham":

> You have called us and we're coming,
>   By Richmond's bloody tide,
> To lay us down for freedom's sake,
>   Our brothers' bones beside. . . .

In "Our Heroes" F. DeHaes Janvier had Northern Americans singing:

> Our patriot soldiers!
> When treason arose,
> And freedom's own children
> Assailed her as foes;
> When anarchy threatened
> And order withdrew,
> They rallied to rescue
> The red, white and blue.
>
> But, glory immortal
> Is waiting them now,
> And chaplets unfading,
> Shall bind every brow;

> When called by the trumpet,
> At time's great review,
> They stand, who defended
> The red, white and blue.

Somewhat later George F. Root, who wrote many war songs for the North, composed "O, Haste on the Battle":

> 'Tis Liberty's battle, and Slavery's death rattle,
> For Freedom shall follow where lately it trod,
> And after the battle, shall man, now a chattel,
> Stand forth in his freedom, the image of God.

In M. L. Hofford's "Dead on the Battle Field," Northerners sang:

> Dead on the battlefield!
> In the cause of truth and right,
> He stood resolved to triumph there
> Or perish in the fight.
> The life blood of his heart,
> With purpose pure and high,
> He freely shed in his country's cause
> When summoned thus to die.[15]

The war rapidly gathered momentum as a crusade for humanitarian principles. Of course, some had so considered it from the very first. Barely two weeks after Sumter one minister told an Eastern audience: "We are called to the defense of *man* against his enemies."[16] In a sermon on *God's Way of Crushing the Rebellion*, George Barrell Cheever said, "God gives us the opportunity to obey and honor him, and to show the beneficent intent and power of the Gospel on a vast scale, in one immediate vast movement, attracting the gaze, gratitude and joy of the world, a movement of justice and humanity for our own good and the happiness of all mankind."[17] In September, 1861, Governor Andrew told the Twentieth Massachusetts Volunteers that they were in a war for humanity.[18] The following spring Senator Benjamin Wade of Ohio proclaimed the war one of despotism against freedom.[19] On an appointed National Fast Day in 1863 many ministers declared that the trials of the war were to make Northerners perfect for their high national mission.[20] In May, 1864, Wendell Phillips addressed the American Anti-Slavery Society at Cooper Institute and said in part, "No sublimer spectacle of intense and disinterested devotion has the world seen for centuries, if ever. On our own soil, each day marks its memory in our minds with the martyrdom of some brave soul in the same cause." He concluded that no obstacle should be permitted to keep the North from securing the rights for which her men fought.[21] At the same time Rufus W. Clark told an Albany audience: "History does not furnish us with an account of any war, which has called forth a purer patriotism, a holier love of liberty, loftier sentiments of honor, duty and devotion to the public good, than have characterized the heroes, who have been engaged and continue to be engaged, in the struggle for the maintenance of the American nationality. In preserving this nationality they have been inspired with the belief that they were toiling to keep alive the best government that Heaven ever granted to a people; to perpetuate and extend those social, educational and religious institutions, upon which virtue and happiness are based, and to secure the triumph of humanity and justice, over systems of oppression, that are a reproach and a peril to any nation."[22] Americans constantly indicated their willingness to die for great humanitarian principles.

In the thirty years before the Civil War, crusading Americans came to expect persecution, and abolitionists had soon learned that their effectiveness increased in direct proportion to the stamina they displayed in suffering for cause. To the persecutions and sacrifices of the Pilgrim fathers, of early dissenters like Roger Williams and the Quakers, of George Washington and his courageous soldiers, of Nathan Hale, the Martyr Spy, of the brave men who in 1812 faced British might to insure American rights in a free sea, they had added the martyr stories of Prudence Crandall, Theodore Weld, James G. Birney, Alanson Work, James Burr, George Thompson, Jonathan Walker, Stephen S. Foster, Parker Pillsbury, Henry B. Stanton, and the rest of the evangelizing Seventy, and of Elijah P. Lovejoy,

Charles T. Torrey, and Old John Brown. Now they added to the list the thousands of Union soldiers who had suffered torture or death at the hands of the Confederates. In the four years of civil strife abolitionists had seen hostility to their agitation turn to patriotic support of the war for freedom. Tertullian had said, "The blood of the martyrs is the seed of the church," and by 1865 American abolitionists well knew it to be true.

But American sacrifice to the Negro's freedom was not yet complete. All during the weary years of fratricidal war a sad-faced man in the White House suffered and died a thousand times as he pondered the devastation of the terrible conflict. His eyes grew sadder and the lines in his face deepened as his every plan to save the Union and end the bloodshed failed and the war continued. When he issued his preliminary Emancipation Proclamation in September, 1862, Abraham Lincoln prayed that its threat would bring back the "erring sisters" and would save the world's greatest experiment in democracy.

But as the South fought on and more and more American lives went to the sacrifice, Abraham Lincoln pondered the human cost of saving the Union. At Gettysburg he said, "We have come to dedicate a portion of that field as a final resting place for those who here gave their lives that that nation might live." The sacrifices mounted for seventeen more months. Then suddenly the nation learned that the fighting had stopped. Robert E. Lee had surrendered to Ulysses S. Grant and the North rejoiced. But joy was short-lived.

On April 15, 1865, the world heard that the President himself had died a victim of the violence which was rampant in the land. As suddenly as the assassin's bullet had struck him down, Abraham Lincoln stood upon the pinnacle of American martyrdom. In the days and weeks that followed, a stunned nation contemplated his life and his death. Hundreds of editors, lecturers, and ministers echoed the truth of his Christlike sacrifice and the legacy of freedom which he left his country and the world.

Said Joseph Medill in the *Chicago Tribune*, "The nation

A Northern newspaper's conception of "Southern inhumanity" to prisoners.

Edwin Stanton fed anti-Southern sentiment with an elaborate funeral procession for Lincoln from Washington to Illinois. Here Chicago celebrates the martyrdom.

mourns. Its agony is great. Its grief is dumb. Never before have the American people been so stricken. Our President has fallen in the prime of his energy and usefulness, another martyr to the demon—Slavery."[23] The black-bordered *Leslie's Illustrated Weekly* proclaimed, "Abraham Lincoln has joined the noble army of Freedom's Martyrs. 'Christ died to make men holy; he died to make men free!' "[24] Ministers remarked of the day on which he died. In Hartford a Baptist clergyman told his people, "Yes, it was meet that the martyrdom should occur on Good Friday. It is no blasphemy against the Son of God and the Saviour of men that we declare the fitness of the slaying of the second Father of our Republic on the anniversary of the day on which He was slain. Jesus Christ died for the world, Abraham Lincoln died for his country."[25] Another Connecticut minister, Thomas P. Field of New London, said: "My friends, in this last appalling tragedy that robbed us of the President, we see a symbol of this conflict that has been going on so long. We see in Lincoln the representative of freedom. . . . But in taking the life of the good man, the friend of freedom, it, thanks be to God, did not destroy freedom itself. . . . We shall hear the name of Lincoln mentioned henceforth as the martyr of Liberty."[26] "A nation at a funeral!" said a clergyman of the same town, "It is even so; and God from on high is looking down on the scene which Himself had ordained for a great and worthy end."[27]

In Philadelphia Frederick Fraley told the Union League: "The words 'It was expedient that one man should die for the people' have been ringing in my ears ever since I heard of the death of the President. These words, I speak it in fear and trembling lest I should err, have filled my heart with a glorious hope for the future; they seem to say to me the blood that has thus been shed shall be a passover for this nation. It shall cleanse us from all malice, from all strife, from all hatred, from all self-sufficiency; it shall teach us to be *just* as well as merciful; it shall make our country a glorious kingdom for the manifestation of those sublime teachings of obedience to law, of charity and peace, and good-will to men, which were given to the world by Him who died on Calvary. It will make our land the land of virtue and freedom; the guiding and ruling star of the whole earth!"[28]

In Buffalo a Presbyterian clergyman told a commemorative meeting that, "Our murdered President has gone to join and complete the glorious roll of our martyrs in this war; to lay his honored dust beside the humblest grave of the humblest soldier of the Republic."[29] "Our Deliverer is made a martyr," cried another eulogist, "but the cause survives: our chieftain is cut off, but the nation and the country continue,"[30] while another proclaimed, "Martyr of liberty, great sacrifice to thy Nation's existence, rest in thy Western grave!"[31] Said the Reverend Phineas D. Gurley, pastor of the Presbyterian church which Lincoln attended in Washington, "He, too, must seal his mission with his blood. He did so seal it."[32]

At a special service conducted by the New York state legislature one member summed up the attitude of the entire nation when he said: "History has recorded in letters of living light the names of those in all ages, of whom the world was not worthy, who were caught up from the loathsome dungeon, from torturing racks, from blazing piles, from the scaffold and the gibbet, to undying fame. She has taught us, by glorious deeds and glorious examples, that many have dared to die for humanity, and in death have found immortality. She has made mankind nobler by such examples of heroism. But scan her pages as we may, search all ancient and all modern lore, read with tear-dimmed eyes the epitaphs of the good and the great of dead generations, yet shall the name of our martyred hero glow as brightly and his deeds be recorded as proudly as any of that long procession who have gone before."[33]

Martyrdom was a revered American tradition. Every American believed that persecution sent the earliest settlers to the continent. All remembered colonial sufferings from British despotism, and the willingness with which the signers of the Declaration of Independence pledged their lives, their fortunes, and their honor in support of the great precepts set forth in that document. They knew that George Washington and the shivering, half-clad patriots of his army had suffered without complaint to save their countrymen from British tyranny and that Nathan Hale had gone to his execution with no regret except that he had but one life to give for his country. Many could remember the suffering and sacrifice of the men who fought for American maritime rights in 1812. By 1830, then, the martyr concept was indeed a vital element in American tradition.

Against this background the hitherto slow-moving campaign against American Negro slavery had suddenly flared as a fiery crusade when in 1831 William Lloyd Garrison brought out the *Liberator* and screamed defiance at the forces which permitted continuance of the infamous institution. Although the abolition movement, initiated by scattered Quakers and other religious people, dated back to colonial days, the organization of numerous antislavery societies had been a quiet activity not particularly striking amongst the stirring political interests of the early days of the republic. With the new publication, however, Garrison's exhortations came as the voice of the prophet. Abolitionists, he declared, would suffer and stand or die for the Negro's freedom. His fellow crusaders had seen that he was right. Their cause needed martyrs to vindicate its righteousness.

So in the three decades before the Civil War, abolitionists demonstrated time after time the truth of Jesus' teaching that no greater love existed than that of the man who would lay down his life for his friends. The mourners for the murdered Lincoln could look back upon a long line of patriots who had suffered for cause; since 1831 abolitionists, in their oft-repeated tales of their suffering and sacrifice, had called upon Americans to note the similarity of their immolation to that of the heroes and heroines of John Foxe's *Book of Martyrs*. Abolition crusaders stood starkly real and dramatic against the American tradition of the martyr concept: Prudence Crandall persecuted and jailed for her determination to educate black girls in a white community; James G. Birney renouncing family, fortune, and friends to battle for his Negro brethren; Theodore Weld, stoned, rotten-egged, beaten, and hooted down until his great vitality waned and his magnificent voice broke; Alanson Work, James Burr, and George Thompson imprisoned in Missouri; Jonathan Walker with his poor branded palm; Stephen S. Foster, Parker Pillsbury, and Henry B. Stanton and all the rest of the evangelizing Seventy driven from place to place; even William Lloyd Garrison whose tussle with a Boston mob might have had more serious consequences. Then, towering above all these, abolition crusaders pointed out three of their band whose sacrifices went beyond all the others: Elijah P. Lovejoy coldly murdered by the Alton mob which opposed his antislavery *Observer,* Charles T. Torrey racked with tuberculosis and then dead in a Maryland jail, John Brown mounting the steps of the crude gibbet on the outskirts of Charles Town after Virginia's summary trial and sentence. In addition, Americans knew, martyrs had suffered and died in the war just ended. Union soldiers suffering torture or death or both were a part of the sacrifice required to advance the great humanitarian principle of freedom.

Suddenly in April, 1865, his countrymen saw that all American martyrdoms for freedom had been but a part of a long prologue to the greatest of them all: the bloody sacrifice of Abraham Lincoln, child of the people. Somehow his death became a fitting, though horrible, climax to a long struggle for various phases of the great humanitarian principle of freedom. Then after a few days many remembered his special qualifications for martyrdom. Born of the people, yet raised to high position, Abraham Lincoln had ever retained his love and respect for his own kind. Through four awful years of war his cavernous eyes had become sadder and the lines in his homely face deeper as his devotion to his people and to the Union he had hoped to mend took every measure of his strength. Then he had died by violence just as he glimpsed the successful completion of his mission. In the rainy April days after Abraham Lincoln's death men sadly shook their heads and murmured that this sad-faced, kindly, enigmatic man was surely the American martyr of martyrs.

The Civil War had once more transferred the struggle against American slavery from an emphasis upon the sin of one man's holding another in bondage to the political and economic implications of the institution. In the process, professional politicians replaced crusading zealots as spokesmen for ways and means of procuring freedom for the Negro. Even before the first shells had sailed into Fort Sumter, men high in political office had assumed the task of enlightening Americans upon that subject. These abolitionist politicians, having witnessed how the repetitious tales of the abolition martyrs had proved the truth of Tertullian's "The blood of the martyrs is the seed of the Church," now quickly seized upon the corpse of The President. Both Edwin M. Stanton, the capable if erratic Secretary of War, and Senator Charles Sumner of Massachusetts who had himself suffered at the hands of slavery's protagonists, as well as their colleagues among the Radical Republicans, well knew wherein the patient and kindly Lincoln had differed from them in their vengeful plans for punishing the South for four years of fratricidal war. And just as well they knew the real grief of any people for one of their own who has died for them. The Radicals saw their course.

Led by the wily Stanton, they laid their plans to emphasize to the American people the sorrowful fact that Abraham Lincoln, risen from the humblest of them, had not only died for love of them but had died as he did because Southerners hated the Union which he had loved and meant to save, that Southern unreason had occasioned the bitter, four-year conflict, that Southern plotters had planned his assassination. Once convinced that such nefariousness was responsible for all their woes, the people, in the Radical plan, could be counted upon to fall in with their schemes for vengeance upon and exploitation of, the late Confederacy. The Radicals laid their plans carefully.

When Mary Lincoln decided that her husband should rest on the Illinois prairie, Stanton quickly charted a funeral route which would bring the dead President home to as many Americans as possible. The artful secretary well knew that by viewing the martyred Lincoln or his funeral train the American people would more fully realize their great grief for one of their own who had died for them. Stanton planned well and the multitudes responded.

As the black-draped train carried him west, Abraham Lincoln's compatriots swarmed to honor him. In those cities and towns where the caravan stopped for a display of the corpse, citizens' committees outdid each other in planning parades, funeral music, and other demonstrations. Thousands filed by the open casket and many wept as they looked upon the sad face of the troubled man from the White House. In areas where the train did not stop to show him, grief-stricken faces lined the right of way, citizens enacted tableaux within sight of the train windows or in the railway stations, and mourning-clad delegations went aboard to lay wreaths, festoons, or mottoes upon the martyr's bier. Indeed, as the train bore him west, Lincoln's mourners were ever more eloquent in their grief, and in their demonstrations increasingly ostentatious. By the time the weary funeral party reached Springfield, thousands of Americans had experienced the deep hurt of a great grief. Many were thinking that they and the country—their country and Abraham Lincoln's country—might have been spared this great loss had the citizens of one section not loved slavery more than they loved the Union. The Radicals had planned both wisely and well.

Meanwhile, ministers, lecturers, and politicians reminded Americans that Abraham Lincoln's martyrdom had left his work unfinished. He had died for freedom and his people, and the very extremity of his sacrifice demanded that his work go on. In Buffalo the Reverend Henry Smith said: "The administration of Abraham Lincoln, the father of a regenerated country, the first martyr President in the cause of American liberty, is at an end: but the holy government of God, and the laws of his glorious and universal empire, still survive. Yea, Christ and the precepts of his blessed gospel still remain. The responsibilities and duties of the living followers of Christ, lifted from him who is now with God, still rest upon us."[34] In Cincinnati the Reverend Maxwell P. Gaddis told an opera house audience: "Is not *his blood* sufficient to put out the remaining fires of treason, and from its lofty eminence, will it not spread o'er all the land until it becomes the cementing bond of eternal fidelity to the Union. . . . The wrongs of liberty culminated in the assassination of Mr. Lincoln. . . . Such a death is to be envied; for he who dies for the *freedom* of man never dies."[35] Soon Americans were hearing time after time that it was perhaps also the will of Providence that hands more earthly than Lincoln's should take up the nation's problems.

In support of this theme Phillips Brooks on April 23, 1865, told the congregation of Philadelphia's Church of the Holy Trinity: "The cause that Abraham Lincoln died for shall grow stronger by his death; stronger and sterner. Stronger to set its pillars deep into the structure of our nation's life; sterner to execute the justice of the Lord upon his enemies. . . . And remember this, that the folly of the Slave power in striking the representative of Freedom, and thinking that thereby it killed Freedom itself, is only a folly that we shall echo if we dare to think that in punishing the Representatives of Slavery who did this deed, we are putting Slavery to death."[36] A Buffalo paper echoed, "Perhaps, in the great design of Providence, for the working out of the consequences of this tremendous struggle to their utmost end, it was needful that this awful tragedy should be enacted, to steel the softened temper of the people, and that Abraham Lincoln, his own great part performed, his fame complete, was laid a costly sacrifice upon the altar of that stern deed."[37] In Lowell, Massachusetts, politician George S. Boutwell said bluntly, "Mr. Lincoln is dead, but the nation lives, and the Providence of God ever continues. No single life was ever yet essential to the life of a nation. This is our consolation and ground for confidence in the future."[38] More mundane hands than those of the Great Martyr were ready to take up the nation's work.

In Washington Stanton, Sumner, and their colleagues among the Radical Republicans were well pleased. They echoed the cry that the Lord had sent Abraham Lincoln to die for the people. But in unifying the nation he had fulfilled his lofty mission. And it was God's way, they explained, to assign temporal problems to temporal hands. They, the men of the martyr's party, were prepared to develop means—commensurate, of course, with the enormity of Southern transgression—of returning men and states to whatever might eventually be their proper place in the Union.

As speakers and writers elevated the Great Martyr to godlike heights, the Republicans set out to convince the nation of their right of stewardship to continue his work. Henceforth they identified all the sacrifices of the war with the selfless patriotism of Abraham Lincoln's Republican party. Even as St. Paul had said centuries before, "What shall we then say to these things? If God *be* for us, who *can* be against us?" a midwestern editor was but echoing all the Radical Republicans when he said in 1866: "The issues raised during the war have not yet been disposed of. From the field of battle they have been transferred to the arena of parties, and their correct settlement there is as essential to the welfare of the nation as the triumph of our armies was to its life. They see the danger that will entail upon us if they now falter in the good work they have so successfully carried on to this time, as when war's calamity filled the country with widows and orphans, they will not falter in finishing up the work they have before them. The man or set of men who aim their blows at the life of the Republican party, are only playing into the hands of its enemies, those enemies who in the time of civil war gave their aid in favor of the nation's foes."[39] He who stood against the Republican party stood as well against Lincoln, even against the great American tradition of martyrdom for righteousness.

So with Abraham Lincoln's death the Radical Republicans claimed the martyr tradition for their own. In the years after 1865 they continued to remind the nation that the principles of the Republican party were those of the great American Martyr of Martyrs. By so doing they prostituted the martyr tradition to support postwar programs far removed from the American quest for either freedom, justice, or humanitarianism.

Notes
Bibliography
Index

Notes

THE MARTYR IN AMERICA

For a discussion of the religious climate of early New England see James T. Adams, *The Founding of New England*, pp. 146–174; Andrews, *The Colonial Period of American History*, 1:470–487; Curti, *The Growth of American Thought*, pp. 69–70; Allen Johnson, ed., *Dictionary of American Biography*, 4:460–462, 9:436–437, 20:286-289, 408–411; Nettels, *The Roots of American Civilization*, pp. 167–179; Parrington, *Main Currents in American Thought*, 1:27–75; Sweet, *Religion in Colonial America;* Wertenbaker, *The First Americans*, pp. 96–104; Wertenbaker, *The Puritan Oligarchy*, pp. 23–24, 41–77, 216–224.

For a discussion of the religious revival in the eighteenth and early nineteenth centuries in America see Curti, *The Growth of American Thought*, pp. 71–78, 120–126, 169–171, 200–204, 306–313; Davidson, *History of the Presbyterian Church*, pp. 133–155; Dimond, *The Psychology of the Methodist Revival*, pp. 18–42, 104–124; Gewehr, *The Great Awakening in Virginia;* Maxson, *The Great Awakening in the Middle Colonies;* Seligman, ed., *Encyclopaedia of the Social Sciences*, 13:365; Sweet, *Revivalism in America*, pp. 24–139; Sweet, *The Story of Religion in America*, pp. 184–223, 322–349; Sweet, *Religion in Colonial America*, pp. 106–108, 271–318; Trollope, *Domestic Manners of the Americans*, 1:104–113, 232–245; Winslow, *Jonathan Edwards*, pp. 135–214, 308–309.

1. Barnes and Dumond, eds. *Letters of Theodore Dwight Weld, Angelina Grimké Weld, and Sarah Grimké*, 1:310. For Weld's life see Benjamin P. Thomas' scholarly, well written *Theodore Weld, Crusader for Freedom*.
2. Pratt, ed., *Fox's Book of Martyrs*, pp. 20, 25, 45, 48, 481, 485–486, 489, 492, 510, 514–515.
3. Adams, *The Founding of New England*, pp. 263–274.
4. Calverton, *The Awakening of America*, pp. 155n, 156n.
5. Bernard Smith, ed., *The Democratic Spirit*, p. 6.
6. Andrews, *The Colonial Period*, 1:487.
7. Richardson, ed., *A Compilation of the Messages and Papers of the*

Presidents, 1:504, 539; Louisville *Western Courier,* December 20, 27, 1813, March 16, 1815.
8. Jonathan Edwards, *The Works of President Edwards,* 4:370, 432, 576.
9. Wesley, *Sermons,* 1:64.
10. Tyerman, *The Life of the Rev. George Whitefield,* 1:303.

PRELUDE TO CRUSADE

For a discussion of antislavery in America see Alice D. Adams, *The Neglected Period of Anti-Slavery in America;* Barnes, *The Antislavery Impulse;* Dumond, *Antislavery Origins of the Civil War;* Dumond, "The Mississippi: Valley of Decision," *Mississippi Valley Historical Review,* 36:3–26 (June, 1949); Goodell, *Slavery and Anti-Slavery;* Locke, *Anti-Slavery in America;* Macy, *The Anti-Slavery Crusade;* Wilson, *History of the Rise and Fall of the Slave Power,* Vol. 1.

1. Locke, *Anti-Slavery in America,* pp. 15–19.
2. *Ibid.,* pp. 24, 27; Woodson, "Anthony Benezet," *Journal of Negro History,* 2:37n, 38, 38n (January, 1917).
3. *National Cyclopaedia of American Biography,* 25:168.
4. Gummere, ed., *The Journal and Essays of John Woolman,* pp. 19–69, 97, 334–347.
5. Julian, "The Rank of Charles Osborn as an Anti-Slavery Pioneer," *Indiana Historical Society Publications,* 2:235–236; Ketring, *Charles Osborn in the Anti-Slavery Movement,* pp. 11–86.
6. *The Life, Travels and Opinions of Benjamin Lundy,* pp. 13–32, 189–312.
7. Benezet, *Views of American Slavery,* p. 59. For a sketch of Benezet's life see *National Cyclopaedia of American Biography,* 5:419.
8. Finney, "How to Change Your Heart," in *Sermons,* pp. 41–49.

HEAR YE THE PROPHET!

Garrison biographical material in this chapter is based on *DAB;* Garrison and Garrison, *William Lloyd Garrison;* Grimké, *William Lloyd Garrison the Abolitionist;* Johnson, *William Lloyd Garrison and His Times;* Swift, *William Lloyd Garrison.*

1. Garrison, *Garrison,* 1:165.
2. *Ibid.,* 1:180.
3. *Ibid.,* 1:214. Abner Kneeland, sometime Universalist clergyman, was at one time an antitheist and later a pantheist. William Ellery Channing, Unitarian minister who served the Federal Street Church in Boston from 1803 until 1842, was the author of several antislavery treatises.
4. *Ibid.,* 1:235.
5. Barnes and Dumond, *Weld-Grimké Letters,* 1:100.
6. Garrison, *Garrison,* 1:333.

7. *Ibid.*, 1:343.
8. *Ibid.*, 1:351.
9. *Ibid.*, 1:370.
10. *Ibid.,* 1:420. In Boston anti-Garrisonites circulated a handbill against him.
11. *Ibid.*, 1:388.
12. *Ibid.*, 1:403–404.
13. *Ibid.*, 1:518–519.
14. Charles C. Burleigh, antislavery lecturer and author, was one of the more eccentric abolitionists. In 1833 Arthur Tappan chose him to edit the *Unionist,* a paper which Tappan established in Brooklyn, Connecticut, as an organ for the defense of Prudence Crandall.
15. For Mayor Theodore Lyman, see *DAB,* 11:518.
16. Garrison, *Garrison,* 2:14.
17. *Ibid.*, 2:21. On the same day a mob in Utica, New York, broke up a meeting of delegates who had assembled to organize a state antislavery society.
18. *Ibid.*, 2:28.
19. *Ibid.*, 2:113.
20. For Henry C. Wright see *National Cyclopaedia of American Biography,* 2:332.
21. For William Goodell and Elizur Wright, see *DAB,* 7:384–385 and 20:548–549, respectively.
22. Garrison, *Garrison,* 2:265–266.
23. *Ibid.*, 2:295.
24. *Ibid.*, 2:410.

THE FIRST MARTYR

Lovejoy biographical material in this chapter is based on the *Alton Observer,* 1836–1837; Edward Beecher, *Narrative of Riots at Alton; DAB;* Lincoln, *Alton Trials;* Joseph C. Lovejoy and Owen Lovejoy, *Memoir of the Rev. Elijah P. Lovejoy; St. Louis Observer,* 1835–1836; Tanner, *History of the Rise and Progress of the Alton Riots;* Tanner, *The Martyrdom of Lovejoy.*

1. Channing, *The Works of William E. Channing,* 2:148.
2. Lovejoy, *Memoir of the Rev. Elijah P. Lovejoy,* pp. 39, 41.
3. *St. Louis Observer,* September 3, 10, 17, 24, October 1, 8, 15, 22, 29, November 19, 1835.
4. Lovejoy, *Memoir of Lovejoy,* p. 128.
5. *Ibid.*, p. 137.
6. *Ibid.*, pp. 156–157.
7. *Ibid.*, p. 177.
8. *Ibid.*, pp. 184–186.
9. *Ibid.*, pp. 228–229.
10. *Ibid.*, pp. 248–250.

11. *Ibid.,* pp. 264, 265.
12. Tanner, *The Martyrdom of Lovejoy,* p. 136.
13. Lovejoy, *Memoir of Lovejoy,* pp. 278–281.
14. *Ibid.,* p. 283.
15. For a contemporary newspaper account of the Lovejoy troubles in Alton see the *Alton Telegraph,* August 16, September 27, November 8, 15, 1837, January 10, 1838.
16. *Liberator,* November 24, 1837. Under the heading "Voice of the Press" Garrison's paper quoted newspapers from all over the country.
17. *Ibid.,* November 24, December 1, 8, 1837, January 12, 1838.
18. Comments from the last five newspapers in this paragraph are from undated clippings from the respective papers, all in "Comments of the Press—1837," a booklet of clippings from Samuel D. Hastings included in Lovejoy category of boxed materials on slavery in the Wisconsin State Historical Society Library, Madison.
19. Root, *A Memorial of the Martyred Lovejoy,* pp. 1, 12, 15–16.
20. Greene, *The Martyr,* pp. 17–18.
21. *Liberator,* December 8, 1837.
22. *Ibid.*
23. *Sixth Annual Report of the Board of Managers of the Massachusetts Anti-Slavery Society,* pp. 33–34.
24. *Fifth Annual Report of the Executive Committee of the American Anti-Slavery Society,* p. 45.
25. *Liberator,* November 24, 1837.
26. Lovejoy, *Memoir of Lovejoy,* pp. 319–320.
27. Phillips, *Speeches, Lectures, and Letters,* p. 6. For a newspaper account of the meeting see *Liberator,* December 8, 1837.
28. *Ibid.,* November 24, December 1, 8, 1837, January 5, 12, 1838.
29. *Emancipator,* March 14, 1839.
30. *Congressional Globe,* 36 Congress, 1 session (1859–1860), Appendix, p. 205.
31. "Tanner's Lovejoy," *The Nation,* 32:264–265 (April 14, 1881).
32. Dimmock, *Lovejoy, An Address Delivered by Thomas Dimmock.*
33. Lovejoy clipping from the New York *Voice,* January 20, 1898, in boxed materials in American biography, Wisconsin State Historical Society Library, Madison.
34. Jameson, *Elijah Parish Lovejoy As A Christian,* pp. 68–75; Clarence E. Lovejoy, *The Lovejoy Genealogy,* p. 169.

WITH STEADY STEP

The story of Prudence Crandall is based on Barnes and Dumond, *Weld-Grimké Letters,* 1:133; John J. Chapman, *William Lloyd Garrison,* pp. 70–73; *DAB;* Garrison, *Garrison,* 1:315–321; Johnson, *Garrison,* pp. 124–127; Larned, *History of Windham County, Connecticut,* 2:490–502; *Liberator,* March 2, July 6, 1833, September 20, 1834; Macy, *The Anti-Slavery*

Crusade, p. 70; May, *Some Recollections of Our Antislavery Conflict*, pp. 40–71; Mumford, ed., *Memoir of Samuel Joseph May*, pp. 148–150; Stanton, *Random Recollections*, p. 39; *National Cyclopaedia of American Biography*, 2:307; Wigham, *The Anti-Slavery Cause in America*, pp. 19–21; Wilson, *History of the Rise and Fall of the Slave Power*, 1:240–246.

Theodore Weld's story is based on Barnes, *The Antislavery Impulse*, pp. 12–13, 79–85, 139, 178–181, 191–197; Barnes and Dumond, *Weld-Grimké Letters*, 1:xvii–xxvi, 15, 206–207, 237–238, 271, 278, 295, 309–310; 2:597–598; Charles Beecher, ed., *Autobiography of Lyman Beecher*, 2:321; William Birney, *James G. Birney and His Times*, pp. 136–137, 151–152; *DAB;* Dumond, *Antislavery Origins of the Civil War*, pp. 40–41, 49, 56–57, 92, 110–111. Thomas, *Theodore Weld.*

The story of James G. Birney is based on Barnes and Dumond, *Weld-Grimké Letters*, 1:132n, 156, 161, 211, 400; William Birney, *James G. Birney and His Times;* Dumond, *Antislavery Origins of the Civil War*, pp. 21–28, 31–36, 53–55; Dumond, ed., *Letters of James Gillespie Birney*, 1:xii–xviii, 14–16, 112, 145, 232–235, 324–325, 408–409; 2:656; Dumond, "The Mississippi: Valley of Decision," *Mississippi Valley Historical Review*, 36:9-10 (June, 1949); Johnson, *Garrison*, pp. 220–222; Macy, *The Anti-Slavery Crusade*, pp. 33–39; *National Cyclopaedia of American Biography*, 2:312; Pillsbury, *Acts of the Anti-Slavery Apostles*, pp. 54–55; Wilson, *History of the Rise and Fall of the Slave Power*, 1:277–279.

1. Birney, *Birney*, p. 152.
2. Barnes and Dumond, *Weld-Grimké Letters*, 1:310.

WEEP NOT FOR ME

For information about George Thompson, Alanson Work, and James E. Burr see *Emancipator and Weekly Chronicle*, February 5, 19, 1845; Goodell, *Slavery and Anti-Slavery*, pp. 440–441; *Liberator*, October 8, November 26, December 10, 17, 1841; Thompson, *Prison Life and Reflections.*

The story of Jonathan Walker is based on *Emancipator and Weekly Chronicle*, August 28, September 11, 18, 25, October 16, November 6, 1844, March 19, July 2, 16, August 6, 1845; Goodell, *Slavery and Anti-Slavery*, p. 439; *Liberator*, October 11, November 22, December 13, 20, 27, 1844, January 3, March 3, July 25, August 1, 15, 23, 29, September 5, 19, 26, October 3, 1845; Walker, *Trial and Imprisonment of Jonathan Walker;* Wilson and Fiske, *Appleton's Cyclopaedia*, 6:328.

1. Thompson, *Prison Life*, pp. 14–15, 19.
2. *Ibid.*, p. 18.
3. *Ibid.*, p. 28.
4. *Liberator*, November 26, 1841.
5. Thompson, *Prison Life*, p. 101.
6. *Liberator*, December 10, 1841.

AS LAMBS AMONG WOLVES

Biographical material on Stephen S. Foster and Parker Pillsbury in this chapter is based on *National Cyclopaedia of American Biography*, 2:328, 330; Pillsbury, *Acts of the Anti-Slavery Apostles*.

1. Pillsbury, *Acts of the Anti-Slavery Apostles,* p. 210.
2. *Ibid.,* pp. 267–272.
3. *Ibid.,* p. 264.
4. *Ibid.,* pp. 346, 347.
5. *Ibid.,* p. 282.
6. *Ibid.,* p. 201.
7. Stanton, *Random Recollections,* pp. 27, 31–34, 52–54.
8. *National Cyclopaedia of American Biography,* 2:313.
9. Wilson, *History of the Rise and Fall of the Slave Power,* 1:280.
10. *National Cyclopaedia of American Biography,* 2:327.
11. Barnes and Dumond, *Weld-Grimké Letters,* 1:260–261, 278–279, 282–285, 298–299.
12. Goodell, *Slavery and Anti-Slavery,* p. 438.
13. *Ibid.,* pp. 437–438.

OF WHOM THEY WERE NOT WORTHY

The story of Charles T. Torrey is based on Blake, *Centurial History of the Mendon Association of Congregational Ministers,* pp. 78, 316–319; *DAB; Emancipator,* 1842, 1844, 1845, 1846; Garrison, *Garrison,* Vol. 2; *Liberator,* 1841, 1844, 1845, 1846; Joseph C. Lovejoy, *Memoir of Rev. Charles T. Torrey; Niles' National Register,* January–February, 1842, February, April, November, 1844.

1. Lovejoy, *Memoir of Torrey,* p. 30.
2. *Ibid.,* p. 32.
3. *Ibid.,* pp. 39–40.
4. *Ibid.,* p. 68.
5. *Ibid.,* p. 60.
6. *Liberator,* June 11, 18, July 2, 1841; *Tenth Annual Report of the Massachusetts Anti-Slavery Society,* pp. 81–82.
7. Lovejoy, *Memoir of Torrey,* p. 95.
8. *Emancipator,* May 27, 1842, July 3, 24, August 7, 1844; *Liberator,* October 22, 1841, September 13, 1844.
9. Lovejoy, *Memoir of Torrey,* pp. 144–145.
10. *Ibid.,* p. 128.
11. *Emancipator and Weekly Chronicle,* July 17, August 28, September 4, 11, October 2, 9, December 11, 25, 1844, January 1, 8, 22, February 12, 26, March 5, April 2, 30, May 17, 21, June 18, October 22, 29, November 5, 1845, February 25, May 27, 1846; *Liberator,* September 6, 13, 27, December 13, 20, 1844, January 3, 10, December 5, 1845, February 21, May 27, 1846.

12. Lovejoy, *Memoir of Torrey*, p. 247.
13. Dumond, *Letters of Birney*, 2:997; *Emancipator*, March 4, May 20, 1846; *Liberator*, February 27, 1846.
14. Dumond, *Letters of Birney*, 2:1007; *Emancipator*, March 4, April 1, 29, May 13, 20, 1846; *Liberator*, April 3, 1846.
15. *Boston Recorder*, May 28, 1846; *Emancipator*, April 1, 8, June 3, 10, 17, November 11, 1846; *Liberator*, January 9, February 27, 1846.
16. *Emancipator*, May 6, 1846.
17. *Ibid.*, April 8, 29, May 13, 1846; *Liberator*, April 24, May 8, 1846.
18. *Boston Recorder*, May 21, 1846; *Emancipator*, May 6, 13, 20, June 24, 1846; *Liberator*, May 8, 1846.
19. *Emancipator*, May 27, 1846.
20. *Baltimore Sun*, May 11, 1846; *Boston Recorder*, May 14, 1846; *Emancipator*, May 13, 20, 27, June 3, 10, 17, 24, July 8, 22, 1846.
21. *Baltimore Sun*, May 18, 1846; *Boston Recorder*, May 21, 1846; *Emancipator*, May 20, 27, June 3, 17, 1846.
22. M. M. Southworth of Lockport, New York, to Lyman C. Draper in Baltimore, January 30, 1846, in Draper Correspondence in Wisconsin State Historical Society Library, Madison.
23. *Emancipator*, January 29, February 5, 11, 19, 26, March 5, 12, 1845, May 20, 27, June 3, 10, 17, 24, July 1, 8, 15, 26, August 12, 26, September 9, 1846; *Liberator*, June 5, 12, July 3, 1846.
24. Martyn, *Wendell Phillips: the Agitator*, p. 219.

APPEAL TO BALLOT AND STATUTE

The account of the abolitionists' association of their cause with the preservation of traditional American rights is based on Charles F. Adams, ed., *Memoirs of John Quincy Adams*, 9:275–276, 302–303, 335, 349–350, 365, 379–380, 388, 397, 443, 448, 460–469; Barnes, *The Antislavery Impulse*, pp. 110–137, 140–143; Barnes and Dumond, *Weld-Grimké Letters*, 2:905–906, 922, 927; *Congressional Globe* for the 23rd through the 29th Congress; Dumond, "The Mississippi: Valley of Decision," *Mississippi Valley Historical Review*, 36:3–26 (June, 1949); *Fifth Annual Report of the American Anti-Slavery Society*, p. 48; Marryatt, *A Diary in America*, 3:80–81; Nevins, *The Diary of Philip Hone*, 2:547–548, 581–583; Nye, *Fettered Freedom*, pp. 4–8, 32–38, 44–46, 54–69; Tyler, *Freedom's Ferment*, pp. 501–508; Thomas, *Theodore Weld*, pp. 129–131.

The account of political abolitionism and the development of legalistic arguments against slavery is based on James T. Adams, *The Adams Family*, pp. 239–242; *Dictionary of American History*, 1:164, 219–220, 442–443; 2:167–168, 333–334, 354–355, 372; 3:197–198, 272, 385–387; 4:80–81, 254–255, 454; 5:337; Dumond, *Antislavery Origins of the Civil War*, pp. 66, 89–97, 115–130; Hesseltine, *Lincoln and the War Governors*, pp. 6–16; Hesseltine, *The Rise and Fall of Third Parties*, pp. 58–62; Hicks, *The Federal Union*, pp. 447–449, 501, 519–522, 525, 532–547, 567–589, 598–604; Nevins,

Ordeal of the Union, pp. 3–121, 301–346, 380–450; Theodore C. Smith, *The Liberty and Free-Soil Parties in the Northwest,* pp. 1–5, 27–260, 285–307, 326–331; Theodore C. Smith, *Parties and Slavery,* pp. 14–27, 94–108, 121–135, 149–173, 190–221, 236–248; Thomas, *Theodore Weld,* pp. 221–223; Williams, *Lincoln and the Radicals,* pp. 4–9.

1. *DAB,* 3:308.
2. Booth and Paine clippings from *Chicago Chronicle,* November 1, 1896, Milwaukee *Sentinel,* January 27, March 12, 1897 and the Milwaukee *Evening Wisconsin,* June 8, 1907, in boxed materials on state history in Wisconsin State Historical Society Library, Madison; Carter, "The Booth War in Ripon," in *Proceedings of the State Historical Society of Wisconsin at its 50th Annual Meeting,* pp. 161–172.

HE BEING DEAD, YET SPEAKETH

The John Brown story told in this chapter is based on Avey, *The Capture and Execution of John Brown;* Chamberlin, *John Brown;* Connelley, *John Brown; DAB;* DuBois, *John Brown;* Hinton, *John Brown and His Men;* Hughes, ed., *Letters and Recollections of John Murray Forbes,* 1:178–182; Jenks, "The John Brown Myth," *The American Mercury,* 1:267–273 (March, 1924); "John Brown and Garrison," *The American,* 11:247–248 (February 6, 1886); Karsner, *John Brown, Terrible 'Saint';* William Lawrence, *Life of Amos Lawrence,* pp. 122–134; *Life, Trial and Execution of Captain John Brown;* Malin, *John Brown and the Legend of Fifty-Six;* New York *Spectator,* October through December, 1859; *New York Tribune,* October through December, 1859; Newton, *Captain John Brown of Harper's Ferry;* Redpath, *Echoes of Harper's Ferry;* Sanborn, "The Great Agitation," *Cosmopolitan Magazine,* 7:52–58 (May, 1889); Sanborn, "John Brown's Family Compact," *The Nation,* 51:500 (December 25, 1890); Sanborn, ed., *The Life and Letters of John Brown;* Sanborn, *Memoirs of John Brown;* Stearns, ed., *John Brown;* Villard, *John Brown;* Warren, *John Brown;* Weisberger, "The Newspaper Reporter and the Kansas Imbroglio," *Mississippi Valley Historical Review,* 36:633–656 (March, 1950).

1. Sanborn, *Life and Letters of John Brown,* p. 13.
2. *Ibid.,* p. 15.
3. Hinton, *John Brown and His Men,* pp. 30–31.
4. *Ibid.,* pp. 585–586.
5. *Ibid.,* p. 19.
6. Gerrit Smith, philanthropist of Peterboro, New York, helped the Kansas Aid and the New England Emigrant Aid societies and John Brown.
7. Karsner, *John Brown,* p. 195.
8. Hinton, *John Brown and His Men,* pp. 619–634.
9. *Life, Trial and Execution of Captain John Brown,* p. 55.

10. Karsner, *John Brown,* p. 313.
11. *Liberator,* November 18, 1859.
12. *New York Tribune,* October 31, December 3, 1859; New York *Independent,* December 8, 1859; Boston *Christian Register,* November 5, December 10, 1859; Chicago *Christian Times and Illinois Baptist,* November 2, 1859.
13. All quoted in *Liberator,* December 2, 1859.
14. *Ibid.,* October 21, 1859.
15. Phillips, *Speeches, Lectures, and Letters,* p. 288; *New York Tribune,* November 3, 1859; Redpath, *Echoes of Harper's Ferry,* p. 118.
16. *National Anti-Slavery Standard,* December 3, 1859.
17. *Liberator,* February 3, 1860.
18. Redpath, *Echoes of Harper's Ferry,* pp. 303–304; Whittier, *Works,* 4:106–107.
19. Redpath, *Echoes of Harper's Ferry,* pp. 39, 120.
20. *New York Tribune,* October 24, 1859.
21. Henry W. Beecher, "The Nation's Duty to Slavery," in John R. Howard, ed., *Patriotic Addresses in England and America,* p. 207.
22. *Liberator,* November 18, 1859.
23. Redpath, *Echoes of Harper's Ferry,* pp. 139, 177, 191, 227, 231.
24. *National Anti-Slavery Standard,* December 3, 1859.
25. Redpath, *Echoes of Harper's Ferry,* pp. 209, 355.
26. *Liberator,* December 30, 1859.
27. *Ibid.,* November 25, 1859.
28. *Ibid.,* December 9, 16, 1859; *New York Tribune,* December 3, 1859.
29. Redpath, *Echoes of Harper's Ferry,* pp. 438, 440–454; *New York Tribune,* December 3, 1859.
30. *Liberator,* December 16, 1859.
31. *Ibid.,* January 27, 1860; *New York Tribune,* December 5, 1859.
32. *Liberator,* November 25, December 16, 23, 31, 1859, January 6, 13, 1860.
33. *New York Tribune,* December 2, 3, 1859; *Liberator,* December 2, 31, 1859, January 13, 1860.
34. Redpath, *Echoes of Harper's Ferry,* p. 383.
35. Villard, *John Brown,* p. 559.
36. *Liberator,* December 2, 31, 1859.
37. Malin, *John Brown and the Legend of Fifty-six,* p. 288.
38. *Liberator,* December 9, 16, 1859, January 6, 1860.
39. *National Anti-Slavery Standard,* January 21, 1860, April 20, 1861.
40. Redpath, *Echoes of Harper's Ferry,* p. 4.
41. Kimball, "Origin of the John Brown Song," *New England Magazine,* New Series, 1:372–374 (December, 1889).
42. Sanborn, *Life and Letters of John Brown,* unnumbered page following viii.
43. *Liberator,* February 19, 1864.
44. *Chicago Tribune,* September 1, 1882.

45. Clippings from *New York Tribune,* November 25, 1883, the *Chicago Times,* December 13, 1883, and from an unidentified, undated paper which quoted the *Springfield Republican,* all in Brown category of boxed materials on slavery in Wisconsin State Historical Society Library, Madison.

46. *Proceedings of the Massachusetts Historical Society,* pp. 181–183, 216.

47. Sanborn, "John Brown's Family Compact," *The Nation,* 51:500 (December 25, 1890).

48. Brown, "Lovejoy's Influence on John Brown," *The Magazine of History,* 23:101 (September–October, 1916).

WHO CAN BE AGAINST US?

The story of Elmer E. Ellsworth is based on *Leslie's Illustrated Magazine,* June 1, 1861; *National Anti-Slavery Standard,* June 1, 1861; New York *Independent,* May 30, June 6, 1861; *New York Tribune,* May 25 through 31, June 1 through 6, 1861.

"Parson" Brownlow's story is based on Brownlow, *Sketches of the Rise, Progress, and Decline of Secession;* Brownlow, *Sufferings of Union Men;* Coulter, *William G. Brownlow, Fighting Parson of the Southern Highlands.*

The account of reported Southern prison and battlefield atrocities is based on Chalmers, *The Storming of Fort Pillow; Encyclopaedia Americana,* 11:506; *Fort Pillow Massacre,* 38 Congress, 1 session, House Report No. 65; *Harper's Weekly,* August, 1861—June, 1862; Percy Howard, *The Barbarities of the Rebels; Leslie's Illustrated Magazine,* May 7, 1864; *New York Times,* July, 1861; *Returned Prisoners,* 38 Congress, 1 session, House Report No. 67; United States Sanitary Commission, *Narrative of Privations and Sufferings of United States Officers and Soldiers.*

Abraham Lincoln material in this chapter is based on *Congressional Globe,* 1861–1866; Eisenschiml, *In the Shadow of Lincoln's Death;* Eisenschiml, *Why Was Lincoln Murdered?;* Hesseltine, *Lincoln and the War Governors;* Lewis, *Myths After Lincoln;* Randall, *The Civil War and Reconstruction;* Sumner, *The Promises of the Declaration of Independence;* Welles, *Diary of Gideon Welles,* 2:283–293, 299–305, 325, 331, 369, 583, 3:45–51, 59–62; Williams, *Lincoln and the Radicals.*

1. *New York Tribune,* April 15, 1861.
2. Quoted *ibid.*
3. New York *Independent,* April 25, 1861.
4. Henry W. Beecher, "The National Flag," in Howard, *Patriotic Addresses,* p. 302.
5. Boston *Christian Register,* April 27, 1861.
6. *New York Tribune,* April 26, 1861.
7. Hanson, *Historical Sketch of the Old Sixth Regiment of Massachusetts Volunteers,* p. 17.

8. Watson, *Addresses, Reviews and Episodes Chiefly Concerning the "Old Sixth" Massachusetts Regiment*, p. 43.

9. *New York Times*, April 23, 1861.

10. *Ibid.*, July 25, 1861.

11. *Harper's Weekly*, December 7, 1861.

12. Julian, *Select Speeches*, p. 7.

13. United States Sanitary Commission, *Narrative of Privations and Sufferings*, pp. 60–61, 73–74.

14. *Leslie's Illustrated Magazine*, May 7, 1864.

15. *Our War Songs North and South*, pp. 126, 393, 409, 419–420.

16. Helmer, *The War Begun*, p. 27.

17. Cheever, *God's Way of Crushing the Rebellion*, p. 8.

18. *Liberator*, September 13, 1861.

19. *Congressional Globe*, 37 Congress, 2 session (1861–1863), p. 1919; *Liberator*, May 23, 1862.

20. Brainerd, *Patriotism Aiding Piety*, pp. 17–19; Stewart, *The Nation's Sins and the Nation's Duty*, p. 15.

21. *Liberator*, May 27, 1864.

22. Clark, *A Discourse Commemorative of the Heroes of Albany*, pp. 7–8.

23. *Chicago Tribune*, April 17, 1865.

24. *Leslie's Illustrated Magazine*, April 29, 1865.

25. Lewis, *Myths After Lincoln*, p. 110.

26. *Funeral Observances at New London*, pp. 32–33.

27. *Ibid.*, pp. 13–14.

28. *Proceedings of the Union League of Philadelphia*, pp. 20–21.

29. *In Memoriam. Abraham Lincoln Assassinated*, p. 30.

30. Henry L. Edwards, *Discourse Commemorative of Our Illustrious Martyr*, p. 15.

31. Frelinghuysen, *Oration at Obsequies of Abraham Lincoln*, pp. 14–15.

32. Gurley, *The Voice of the Rod*, p. 12.

33. *Legislative Honors to the Memory of President Lincoln*, pp. 45–46.

34. *In Memoriam. Abraham Lincoln Assassinated*, p. 26.

35. Gaddis, *Sermon Upon the Assassination of Abraham Lincoln*, pp. 9, 11, 13.

36. Brooks, *The Life and Death of Abraham Lincoln*, p. 21.

37. Quoted in *In Memoriam. Abraham Lincoln Assassinated*, p. 13.

38. Boutwell, *Eulogy on the Death of Abraham Lincoln*, p. 17.

39. *Peoria (Illinois) Transcript*, June 9, 1866.

Bibliography

Abel, Annie H., and Klingberg, Frank J., eds. *A Side-Light on Anglo-American Relations, 1839–1858.* Lancaster, Pennsylvania, 1927.

Adams, Alice D. *The Neglected Period of Anti-Slavery in America (1808–1831).* Boston, 1908.

Adams, Charles Francis, ed. *Memoirs of John Quincy Adams Comprising Portions of His Diary from 1795 to 1848.* 12 vols. Philadelphia, 1874.

Adams, James T. *The Adams Family.* New York, 1930.

———. *The Founding of New England.* Boston, 1921.

Alton Observer, 1836–1837.

Alton Telegraph, 1837–1838.

Andrews, Charles M. *The Colonial Period of American History.* 4 vols. New Haven, 1934–1938.

Annual Report of the American Anti-Slavery Society, by the Executive Committee, for the Year Ending May 1, 1860. New York, 1861.

Avey, Elijah. *The Capture and Execution of John Brown. A Tale of Martyrdom.* Chicago, 1906. The author presents himself as an eyewitness to the events he chronicles.

Baltimore Sun, 1846.

Barnes, Gilbert H. *The Antislavery Impulse 1830–1844.* New York, 1933.

——— and Dumond, Dwight L., eds. *Letters of Theodore Dwight Weld, Angelina Grimké Weld, and Sarah Grimké 1822–1844.* 2 vols. New York, 1934.

Beardsley, Frank G. *A Mighty Winner of Souls, Charles G. Finney. A Study in Evangelism.* New York, 1937.

Beecher, Charles, ed. *Autobiography, Correspondence, etc. of Lyman Beecher.* 2 vols. New York, 1865.

Beecher, Edward. *Narrative of Riots at Alton in Connection with the Death of Rev. Elijah P. Lovejoy.* Alton, 1838.

Benezet, Anthony. *A Caution to Great Britain and Her Colonies, in a Short Representation of the Calamitous State of the Enslaved Negroes in the British Dominions.* Philadelphia, 1784.

————. *A Short Account of that Part of Africa Inhabited by the Negroes*. Philadelphia, 1762. This is not only an account of the country and the natives, but also an attempt to show the wrong of slave trade and to refute proslavery arguments.

————. *Some Historical Account of Guinea, its Situation, Produce and the General Disposition of its Inhabitants. With an Inquiry into the Rise and Progress of the Slave Trade, its Nature, and Lamentable Effects*. London, 1788. Describes Africa, gives antislavery arguments, and exposes cruelty of the slave trade.

————. *Views of American Slavery Taken A Century Ago*. Philadelphia, 1858.

Biographical Directory of the American Congress 1774–1927. Washington, 1928.

Birney, Catherine. *The Grimké Sisters*. Boston, 1885.

Birney, James G. *The American Churches the Bulwarks of American Slavery*. Newburyport, 1842.

Birney, William. *James G. Birney and His Times. The Genesis of the Republican Party With Some Account of Abolition Movements in the South Before 1828*. New York, 1890.

Blake, Mortimer. *Centurial History of the Mendon Association of Congregational Ministers with the Centennial Address, Delivered at Franklin, Mass., Nov. 19, 1851, and Biographical Sketches of Members and Licentiates*. Boston, 1853.

Boston *Christian Register*, 1859, 1861.

Boston Recorder, 1846.

Boutwell, George S. *Eulogy on the Death of Abraham Lincoln. Delivered Before the City Council and Citizens of Lowell at Huntington Hall, April 19, 1865*. Lowell, 1865.

Brainerd, Thomas. *Patriotism Aiding Piety. A Sermon Preached in the Third Presbyterian Church, Philadelphia, April 30, 1863*. Philadelphia, 1863.

Brookes, George S. *Friend Anthony Benezet*. Philadelphia, 1937.

Brooks, Phillips. *The Life and Death of Abraham Lincoln. A Sermon Preached at the Church of the Holy Trinity, Philadelphia. Sunday morning, April 23, 1865*. Philadelphia, 1865.

Brown, Justus N. "Lovejoy's Influence on John Brown," *The Magazine of History*, 23:97–102 (September–October, 1916).

Brownlow, William G. *Sketches of the Rise, Progress, and Decline of Secession; with a Narrative of Personal Adventures Among the Rebels*. Philadelphia, 1862.

————. *Sufferings of Union Men. An Address Delivered Before Citizens of New York at the Academy of Music May 15, 1862*. n.p., n.d.

Cabot, James E. *A Memoir of Ralph Waldo Emerson*. 2 vols. Boston, 1888.

Calverton, V. F. *The Awakening of America*. New York, 1939.

Carter, George W. "The Booth War in Ripon." *Proceedings of the State Historical Society of Wisconsin at its 50th Annual Meeting.* Madison, 1903.

Chalmers, James R. *The Storming of Fort Pillow.* Washington, 1879.

Chamberlin, Joseph E. *John Brown.* Boston, 1899.

Channing, William E. *The Works of William E. Channing.* 6 vols. Boston, 1845.

Chapman, John J. *William Lloyd Garrison.* Boston, 1921.

Chapman, Maria W. *Right and Wrong in Massachusetts.* Boston, 1840.

Cheever, George B. *God's Way of Crushing the Rebellion. A Sermon Preached in the Church of the Puritans, New York.* New York, 1861.

Chicago *Christian Times and Illinois Baptist,* 1859.

Chicago Chronicle. Clipping dated November 1, 1896, included in Booth category of boxed materials on state history in Wisconsin State Historical Society Library, Madison.

Chicago Times. Clipping dated December 13, 1883, included in Brown category of boxed materials on slavery in Wisconsin State Historical Society Library, Madison.

Chicago Tribune. April–May, 1865, September, 1882 and an undated clipping from Brown category of boxed materials on slavery in Wisconsin State Historical Society Library, Madison.

Clark, Rufus W. *A Discourse Commemorative of the Heroes of Albany, Who Have Fallen During the Present War in Defense of Our Country.* Albany, 1864.

Clarkson, Thomas. *The History of the Rise, Progress, and Accomplishment of the Abolition of the African Slave-Trade by the British Parliament.* 2 vols. London, 1808.

"Comments of the Press—1837," a booklet of clippings from Samuel D. Hastings included in Lovejoy category of boxed materials on slavery in Wisconsin State Historical Society Library, Madison. See especially clipping dated December 5, 1837 from Carlile (Pennsylvania) *Herald* and undated clippings from Gettysburg *Star and Republican Banner,* Homer (New York) *Republican and Eagle,* Louisville (Kentucky) *Herald, Massachusetts Spy,* New York *Observer.*

Congressional Globe, 1834–1846 and 1859–1866.

Connelley, William E. *John Brown.* Topeka, 1900.

The Constitution of the American Anti-Slavery Society: with the Declaration of the National Anti-Slavery Convention at Philadelphia, December, 1833 and the Address to the Public, Issued by the Executive Committee of the Society in September, 1835. New York, 1838.

Coulter, E. Merton. *William G. Brownlow, Fighting Parson of the Southern Highlands.* Chapel Hill, 1937.

Curti, Merle. *The Growth of American Thought*. New York, 1943.

Davidson, Robert. *History of the Presbyterian Church in the State of Kentucky With a Preliminary Sketch of the Churches in the Valley of Virginia*. New York, 1847.

Dedication of the Lovejoy Monument, Alton, Illinois, November 8, 1897. Alton, n.d.

Dimmock, Thomas. *Lovejoy. An Address Delivered by Thomas Dimmock at the Church of the Unity, St. Louis, March 14, 1888*. n.p., n.d.

Dimond, Sidney G. *The Psychology of the Methodist Revival*. London, 1926.

Draper, Lyman. Correspondence in the files of the Wisconsin State Historical Society Library, Madison.

DuBois, W.E.B. *John Brown*. American Crisis Biographies. Philadelphia, 1909.

Dumond, Dwight L. *Antislavery Origins of the Civil War in the United States*. Ann Arbor, 1939.

———. "The Mississippi: Valley of Decision," *Mississippi Valley Historical Review*, 36:3–26 (June, 1949).

———., ed. *Letters of James Gillespie Birney 1831–1857*. 2 vols. New York, 1938.

Edwards, Henry L. *Discourse Commemorative of Our Illustrious Martyr, Delivered in Congregational Church, South Abington, Fast Day, June 1, 1865*. Boston, 1865.

Edwards, Jonathan. *The Works of President Edwards in Four Volumes. A Reprint of the Worcester Edition, with Valuable Additions and a Copious General Index to Which, for the First Time, Has Been Added, at Great Expense, A Complete Index of Scripture Texts*. New York, 1851.

Eisenschiml, Otto. *In the Shadow of Lincoln's Death*. New York, 1940.

———. *Why was Lincoln Murdered?* Boston, 1937.

Emancipator, 1835, 1839, 1842, 1844–1847. This paper briefly bore the title *Emancipator and Weekly Chronicle*.

Fifth Annual Report of the Executive Committee of the American Anti-Slavery Society. New York, 1838.

Finney, Charles G. "How to Change Your Heart." *Sermons*, No. II. New York, February, 1835.

———. *Lectures on Systematic Theology Embracing Lectures on Moral Government*. Oberlin, 1846.

———. *Memoirs of Rev. Charles G. Finney*. New York, 1876.

———. *Sermons on Various Subjects*. New York, 1834.

Fletcher, Robert S. *A History of Oberlin College*. 2 vols. Oberlin, 1943.

Ford, Thomas. *A History of Illinois from its Commencement as a State in 1818 to 1847*. Chicago, 1854.

Fort Pillow Massacre. 38 Congress, 1 session, House Report No. 65. Washington, 1864.

Foster, Frank H. *A Genetic History of the New England Theology.* Chicago, 1907.

Frelinghuysen, Frederick T. *Oration at Obsequies of Abraham Lincoln in Newark, N. J., April 19, 1865.* Newark, 1865.

Funeral Observances at New London, Connecticut in Honor of Abraham Lincoln, Sixteenth President of the United States, Wednesday, April 19, 1865, including the Public Addresses of Rev. G. B. Willcox, and Rev. Thomas P. Field, D.D. New London, 1865.

Gaddis, Maxwell P. *Sermon Upon the Assassination of Abraham Lincoln.* Cincinnati, 1865.

Garrison, Wendell P., and Garrison, Francis J. *William Lloyd Garrison, 1805–1879. The Story of His Life Told by His Children.* 4 vols. New York, 1885.

Genius of Universal Emancipation. November 9, 1838.

Gewehr, Wesley M. *The Great Awakening in Virginia, 1740–1790.* Durham, 1930.

Goodell, William. *Slavery and Anti-Slavery; A History of the Great Struggle in Both Hemispheres; With a View of the Slavery Question in the United States.* New York, 1855.

Greene, Beriah. *The Martyr. A Discourse in Commemoration of the Martyrdom of the Rev. Elijah P. Lovejoy.* New York, 1838.

Grimké, Archibald H. *William Lloyd Garrison, The Abolitionist.* American Reformers Series. New York, 1891.

Gummere, Amelia M., ed. *The Journal and Essays of John Woolman.* New York, 1922.

Gurley, Phineas D. *The Voice of the Rod. A Sermon Preached on Thursday, June 1, 1865, in the New York Avenue Presbyterian Church, Washington, D. C.* Washington, 1865.

Haller, William. *The Rise of Puritanism or, The Way to the New Jerusalem As Set Forth in Pulpit and Press from Thomas Cartwright to John Lilburne and John Milton, 1570–1643.* New York, 1938.

Hanson, John W. *Historical Sketch of the Old Sixth Regiment of Massachusetts Volunteers, During its Three Campaigns in 1861, 1862, 1863, and 1864.* Boston, 1866.

Harper's Weekly, 1859, 1861–1862.

Helmer, C. D. *The War Begun.* Milwaukee, 1861.

Henningsen, C. F. *Letter from Gen. C. F. Henningsen, in Reply to the Letter of Victor Hugo on the Harper's Ferry Invasion with an Extract from the Letter of the Rev. Nathan Lord, D.D., President of Dartmouth College, N. H.; and an Article from the London "Times" on Slavery.* New York, 1860.

Hesseltine, William B. *Lincoln and the War Governors*. New York, 1948.
———. *The Rise and Fall of Third Parties*. Washington, 1948.
Hicks, John D. *The Federal Union*. Cambridge, 1937.
Hinton, Richard J. *John Brown and His Men, With Some Account of the Roads They Traveled to Reach Harper's Ferry*. American Reformers Series. New York, 1894.
Howard, John R., ed. *Patriotic Addresses in America and England, from 1850 to 1885, on Slavery, the Civil War, and the Development of Civil Liberty in the United States*. New York, 1887.
Howard, Percy. *The Barbarities of the Rebels, as Shown in Their Cruelty to the Federal Wounded and Prisoners: in Their Outrages Upon Union Men; in the Murder of Negroes, and in Their Unmanly Conduct Throughout the Rebellion*. Providence, 1863.
Hughes, Sarah Forbes, ed. *Letters and Recollections of John Murray Forbes*. 2 vols. Boston, 1899.
In Memoriam. Abraham Lincoln Assassinated at Washington, April 14, 1865: Being a Brief Account of the Proceedings, Action of Authorities and Societies, Speeches, Sermons, Addresses and Other Expressions of Public Feeling on Reception of the News, and at the Funeral Obsequies of the President, at Buffalo, N. Y. Buffalo, 1865.
Jackson, Samuel M., ed. *The New Schaff-Herzog Encyclopedia of Religious Knowledge*. 12 vols. New York, 1911.
Jameson, Melvin. *Elijah Parish Lovejoy As A Christian*. Rochester, 1910.
Jenks, Leland H. "The John Brown Myth," *The American Mercury*, 1:267–273 (March, 1924).
"John Brown and Garrison," *The American*, 11:247–248 (February 6, 1886).
Johnson, Oliver. *William Lloyd Garrison and His Times; or, Sketches of the Anti-Slavery Movement in America, and of the Man Who Was Its Founder and Moral Leader*. Boston, 1881.
Julian, George W. "The Rank of Charles Osborn As An Anti-Slavery Pioneer," *Indiana Historical Society Publications*, Vol. 2, No. 6. Indianapolis, 1891.
———. *Select Speeches*. Cincinnati, 1867.
Karsner, David. *John Brown, Terrible 'Saint.'* New York, 1934.
Ketring, Ruth A. *Charles Osborn in the Anti-Slavery Movement*. Columbus, 1937.
Kimball, George. "Origin of the John Brown Song," *New England Magazine*. New Series, 1:371–376 (December, 1889).
Lanman, Charles. *Biographical Annals of the Civil Goverment of the United States, During Its First Century*. Washington, 1876.
Larned, Ellen D. *History of Windham County, Connecticut*. 2 vols. Worcester, 1880.

Lawrence, George A. *A Pioneer of Freedom. An Address Delivered Before the Fourteenth Annual Meeting of the Illinois Historical Society Upon the Life and Services of Benjamin Lundy. Delivered in the Senate Chamber at Springfield, Illinois Thursday Evening, May 15, 1913*. n.p., n.d.

Lawrence, William. *Life of Amos Lawrence With Extracts from His Diary and Correspondence*. New York, 1899.

Legislative Honors to the Memory of President Lincoln. Message of Gov. Fenton to the Legislature, Communicating the Death of President Lincoln. Obsequies of President Lincoln in the Legislature. Albany, 1865.

Leslie's Illustrated Weekly, 1861, 1864, 1865.

Lewis, Lloyd. *Myths After Lincoln*. New York, 1929.

Liberator, 1833–1842, 1844–1846, 1859–1862, 1864.

The Life, Travels and Opinions of Benjamin Lundy, Including His Journeys to Texas and Mexico; With a Sketch of Cotemporary Events, and a Notice of the Revolution in Hayti. Compiled Under the Direction and on Behalf of His Children. Philadelphia, 1847.

Life, Trial and Execution of Captain John Brown Known as "Old Brown of Ossawatomie," with a Full Account of the Attempted Insurrection at Harper's Ferry. New York, 1859.

Lincoln, William S. *Alton Trials*. New York, 1838.

Linder, Usher F. *Reminiscences of the Early Bench and Bar of Illinois*. Chicago, 1879.

Locke, Mary S. *Anti-Slavery in America from the Introduction of African Slaves to the Prohibition of the Slave Trade (1619–1808)*. Boston, 1901.

Louisville *Western Courier*, December 20, 27, 1813; March 16, 1815.

Lovejoy, Clarence E. *The Lovejoy Genealogy With Biographies and History 1460–1930*. New York, 1930.

Lovejoy, Joseph C. *Memoir of Rev. Charles T. Torrey Who Died in the Penitentiary of Maryland Where He Was Confined for Showing Mercy to the Poor*. Boston, 1847.

———, and Lovejoy, Owen. *Memoir of the Rev. Elijah P. Lovejoy Who Was Murdered in Defence of the Liberty of the Press, at Alton, Illinois, November 7, 1837*. New York, 1838.

Ludlum, Robert P. "Joshua R. Giddings, Radical." *Mississippi Valley Historical Review*, 23:49–60 (June, 1936).

Macy, Jesse. *The Anti-Slavery Crusade. A Chronicle of the Gathering Storm*. Chronicles of America, Vol. 28. New Haven, 1919.

Malin, James C. *John Brown and the Legend of Fifty-Six*. Philadelphia, 1942.

Marryatt, Frederick. *A Diary in America with Remarks on its Institutions*. 3 vols. London, 1839.

Martyn, Carlos. *Wendell Phillips: the Agitator*. American Reformers Series. New York, 1890.

Maxson, Charles H. *The Great Awakening in the Middle Colonies.* Chicago, 1920.

May, Samuel J. *Some Recollections of Our Antislavery Conflict.* Boston, 1869.

Milwaukee *Evening Wisconsin.* Clipping dated June 8, 1907, included in Paine category of boxed materials on state history in Wisconsin State Historical Society Library, Madison.

Milwaukee *Sentinel.* Clippings dated January 27 and March 12, 1897, included in Paine category of boxed materials on state history in Wisconsin State Historical Society Library, Madison.

Mumford, Thomas J., ed. *Memoir of Samuel Joseph May.* Boston, 1873.

Nettels, Curtis P. *The Roots of American Civilization.* New York, 1940.

Nevins, Allan. *The Diary of Philip Hone 1828–1851.* 2 vols. New York, 1936.

———. *Ordeal of the Union.* New York, 1947.

Newton, John. *Captain John Brown of Harper's Ferry.* New York, 1909.

New York *Independent,* 1859, 1861.

New York *National Anti-Slavery Standard,* 1859–1861.

New York *Spectator,* 1859.

New York Times, 1861.

New York Tribune, 1859, 1861. Also includes clipping dated November 25, 1883, in Brown category of boxed materials on slavery in Wisconsin State Historical Society Library, Madison.

New York *Voice.* Clipping dated January 20, 1898, from Lovejoy clippings in boxed materials on American biography in Wisconsin State Historical Society Library, Madison.

Niles' National Register. Containing Political, Historical, Geographical, Scientific, Statistical, Economical, and Biographical Documents, Essays, and Facts: Together with Notices of the Arts and Manufactures and a Record of the Events of the Times. 1842, 1844–1845. The *Register* was published weekly, first in Washington, then, after 1839, in Baltimore.

Nye, Russel B. *Fettered Freedom.* East Lansing, 1949.

"An Old Play on John Brown." *Kansas Historical Quarterly,* 6:34–59 (February, 1937).

Our War Songs North and South. Cleveland, 1887.

Parrington, Vernon L. *Main Currents in American Thought.* 3 vols. New York, 1927–1930.

Pearson, Henry G. *The Life of John Andrew Governor of Massachusetts 1861–5.* 2 vols. Boston, 1904.

Peoria (Illinois) *Transcript,* June 9, 15, 1866.

Phillips, Wendell. *The Freedom of Speech.* Boston, 1890.

———. *Speeches, Lectures, and Letters.* Boston, 1884.

Pierce, Edward L. *Memoir and Letters of Charles Sumner.* 4 vols. Boston, 1893.

Pillsbury, Parker. *Acts of the Anti-Slavery Apostles.* Boston, 1884.

Pratt, T., ed. *Fox's Book of Martyrs; or, the Acts and Monuments of the Christian Church; Being a Complete History of the Lives, Sufferings, and Deaths of the Christian Martyrs; from the Commencement of Christianity to the Present Period to Which is Added An Account of the Inquisition, the Bartholomew Massacre in France, the General Persecution Under Louis XIV, the Massacres in the Irish Rebellions in the Years 1641 and 1798, Rise, Progress and Persecutions of the People Commonly called Quakers, Together With an Account of the Western Martyrology, or Bloody Assizes with Lives of Some of the Early Eminent Reformers.* Philadelphia, 1856.

Proceedings of the Massachusetts Historical Society 1884–1885. Boston, 1885.

Proceedings of the State Historical Society of Wisconsin at its 50th Annual Meeting. Madison, 1903.

Proceedings of the Union League of Philadelphia, Regarding the Assassination of Abraham Lincoln, President of the United States. Philadelphia, 1865.

Randall, James G. *The Civil War and Reconstruction.* Chicago, 1937.

Redpath, James. *Echoes of Harper's Ferry.* Boston, 1860.

Report of the Boston Female Anti-Slavery Society; With a Concise Statement of Events, Previous and Subsequent to the Annual Meeting of 1835. Boston, 1836.

Returned Prisoners. 38 Congress, 1 session, House Report no. 67. Washington, 1864.

Richardson, James D., ed. *A Compilation of the Messages and Papers of the Presidents 1789–1897.* 10 vols. Washington, 1897.

Riley, Elihu S. *A History of Anne Arundel County in Maryland.* Annapolis, 1905.

Root, David. *A Memorial of the Martyred Lovejoy. A Sermon Delivered in Dover, N.H.* n.p., n.d.

St. Louis Observer, 1835.

Sanborn, Franklin B. *Dr. Samuel G. Howe the Philanthropist.* New York, 1891.

———. "The Great Agitation," *Cosmopolitan Magazine,* 7:52–58 (May, 1889).

———. "John Brown's Family Compact," *The Nation,* 51:500 (December 25, 1890).

———. *Memoirs of John Brown.* Concord, 1878.

———. *Recollections of Seventy Years.* 2 vols. Boston, 1900.

———, ed. *The Life and Letters of John Brown, Liberator of Kansas, and Martyr of Virginia.* Boston, 1885.

Scharf, J. Thomas. *History of Maryland.* 3 vols. Baltimore, 1879.

Shotwell, Walter G. *Life of Charles Sumner.* New York, 1910.

Sixth Annual Report of the Board of Managers of the Massachusetts Anti-Slavery Society. Boston, 1838.

A Sketch of the Condition and Prospects of the Oneida Institute. Utica, 1834.

Smith, Bernard, ed. *The Democratic Spirit. A Collection of American Writings from the Earliest Times to the Present Day.* New York, 1941.

Smith, Theodore C. *The Liberty and Free-Soil Parties in the Northwest.* New York, 1897.

———. *Parties and Slavery.* New York, 1906.

Stanton, Henry B. *Random Recollections.* New York, 1886.

Stearns, Frank P. *The Life and Public Services of George Luther Stearns.* Philadelphia, 1907.

———, ed. *John Brown.* Boston, 1889.

Stewart, William B. *The Nation's Sins and the Nation's Duty.* Philadelphia, 1863.

Stowe, Harriet Beecher. *The Lives and Deeds of Our Self-Made Men.* Boston, 1872.

Sturge, John. *A Visit to the United States in 1841.* Boston, 1842.

Sumner, Charles. *The Promises of the Declaration of Independence. Eulogy on Abraham Lincoln Delivered Before the Municipal Authorities of the City of Boston, June 1, 1865.* Boston, 1865.

Sweet, William W. *Religion in Colonial America.* New York, 1942.

———. *Revivalism in America Its Origin, Growth and Decline.* New York, 1944.

———. *The Story of Religion in America.* New York, 1930.

Swift, Lindsay. *William Lloyd Garrison.* Philadelphia, 1911.

Tanner, Henry. *History of the Rise and Progress of the Alton Riots Culminating in the Death of Rev. Elijah P. Lovejoy, Nov. 7, 1837.* Buffalo, 1878.

———. *The Martyrdom of Lovejoy. An Account of the Life, Trials, and Perils of Rev. Elijah P. Lovejoy Who Was Killed by a Pro-Slavery Mob, at Alton, Ill., on the Night of Nov. 7, 1837. By an Eye Witness.* Chicago, 1881.

"Tanner's Lovejoy," *The Nation,* 32:264–265 (April, 1881).

Tappan, Lewis. *The Life of Arthur Tappan.* New York, 1871.

Tenth Annual Report of the Massachusetts Anti-Slavery Society. Boston, 1842.

Thomas, Benjamin P. *Theodore Weld, Crusader for Freedom.* New Brunswick, 1950.

Thompson, George. *Prison Life and Reflections or A Narrative of the Arrest, Trial, Conviction, Imprisonment, Treatment, Observations, Reflections and Deliverance of Work, Burr, and Thompson Who Suffered an Unjust and Cruel Imprisonment in Missouri*

Penitentiary for Attempting to Aid Some Slaves to Liberty. Dayton, 1860.

The Trial of Reuben Crandall, M.D. Charged with Publishing Seditious Libels, by Circulating the Publications of the American Anti-Slavery Society. Before the Circuit Court for the District of Columbia, Held at Washington in April, 1836, Occupying the Court the Period of Ten Days. New York, 1836.

Trollope, Mrs. Frances. *Domestic Manners of the Americans.* 2 vols. New York, n.d.

Tyerman, Luk. *The Life of the Rev. George Whitefield.* 2 vols. New York, 1877.

Tyler, Alice F. *Freedom's Ferment.* Minneapolis, 1944.

United States Sanitary Commission. *Narrative of Privations and Sufferings of United States Officers and Soldiers While Prisoners of War in the Hands of the Rebel Authorities. Being the Report of a Commission of Inquiry Appointed by the United States Sanitary Commission.* Philadelphia, 1864. An 1865 edition, issued by the Loyal Publication Society, included pictures of Northern men who had suffered in Southern prisons.

Villard, Oswald G. *John Brown 1800–1859; A Biography Fifty Years After.* New York, 1943.

Walker, Jonathan. *Trial and Imprisonment of Jonathan Walker, at Pensacola, Florida, for Aiding Slaves to Escape from Bondage.* Boston, 1846.

Warren, Robert Penn. *John Brown. The Making of a Martyr.* New York, 1929.

Watson, Benjamin F. *Addresses, Reviews and Episodes Chiefly Concerning the "Old Sixth" Massachusetts Regiment.* New York, 1901.

Weeks, Stephen B. *Southern Quakers and Slavery. A Study in Institutional History.* Johns Hopkins University Studies in Historical and Political Science. Extra volume XV. Baltimore, 1896.

Weisberger, Bernard A. "The Newspaper Reporter and the Kansas Imbroglio," *Mississippi Valley Historical Review,* 36:633–656 (March, 1950).

Weld, Theodore D. *American Slavery As It Is. Testimony by a Thousand Witnesses.* New York, 1839. This book is a collection of atrocity stories.

———. *The Bible Against Slavery. An Inquiry into the Patriarchal and Mosaic Systems on the Subject of Human Rights.* New York, 1838.

———. *The Power of Congress over the District of Columbia.* New York, 1838.

Welles, Gideon. *Diary of Gideon Welles.* 3 vols. New York, 1911.

Wertenbaker, Thomas J. *The First Americans 1607–1690.* New York, 1927.

———. *The Puritan Oligarchy.* New York, 1947.

Wesley, John. *Sermons on Several Occasions*. 2 vols. London, 1864.

Whitney, Janet. *John Woolman American Quaker*. Boston, 1942.

Whittier, John G. "The Antislavery Convention of 1833." *Atlantic Monthly*, 33:166–172 (February, 1874).

———. *The Poetical Works of John Greenleaf Whittier in Four Volumes*. 4 vols. New York, 1892.

Wigham, Eliza. *The Anti-Slavery Cause in America and Its Martyrs*. London, 1863.

Williams, T. Harry. *Lincoln and the Radicals*. Madison, 1941.

Wilson, Henry. *History of the Rise and Fall of the Slave Power in America*. 3 vols. Boston, 1872.

Wingate, James. *Wingate's Maryland Register for 1874–'75–'76. A Legal, Political and Business Manual*. Baltimore, 1875.

Winslow, Ola E. *Jonathan Edwards 1703–1758*. New York, 1940.

Woodson, Carter G. "Anthony Benezet," *Journal of Negro History*, 2:37–50 (January, 1917).

Woolman, John. *The Journal of John Woolman with an Introduction by John G. Whittier*. Boston, 1873.

Index

North Elba, N. Y., 112, 115, 128, 130
Northfield, N. H., 77
Northwest Territory: slavery prohibited in, 15
Norwich, Mass., 65, 76

O, Haste on the Battle," song, 142
Oberlin College, 96
Observer: founded, 34; Lovejoy's editorial policy questioned by moderates, 35-37, 38-42; moved from St. Louis to Alton, 38; Lovejoy offers to surrender editorship, 39-40, 41
Ohio, 59, 108; early antislavery activity in, 13, 15; abolitionist activity in, 77-78
Old South Church, Boston, Mass., 125
Oldtown, Ohio: Weld in, 56
Oneida Institute, 21, 55
Osborn, Charles, 78; opposes slavery, 12-13; characterized as martyr, 15
"Our Heroes," song, 141-42

PAINE, Byron, 107
Painesville, Ohio: Weld in, 56-57
Palmyra, Mo.: and abolitionists, 62-64
Parker, Theodore, 105; and John Brown, 115
Park Street Congregational Church, Boston, Mass., 95, 98
Paul, Saint, 7, 8, 62, 64, 65, 78, 152
Payne, J. H., 57
Pennsylvania: early antislavery activity in, 13; outlaws slavery, 15
Pensacola, Fla., 65, 66
Persecution, of early Christians, 4
Personal liberty laws, 60, 107
Peter, Saint, 4, 7
Peterboro, N. Y., 117
Petition, right of, 58, 83; abolitionists and, 100

Petitions, antislavery, 15; sent to Congress by Quakers, 12; distributed by Lovejoy, 38; opposed by South, 100
Phelps, Amos A., abolitionist, 48, 77, 92
Philadelphia, Pa., 14, 20, 47-48, 51, 124, 145, 151; Garrison in, 24
Philanthropist, The, 13, 14
Phillips, Wendell, 105, 129; on Lovejoy's martyrdom, 48; on Torrey's martyrdom, 98; on John Brown's martyrdom, 122, 125; on Civil War as moral crusade, 143
Phillips, William A.: on John Brown's martyrdom, 128
Phillips Exeter Academy, 81
Pierce, Franklin, 106; in election of 1852, 105
Pierpont, John, 91
Pillsbury, Parker, 97, 98, 128, 148; abolitionist activity, 70ff.
Pittsburg Times: on Weld, 54
Plymouth, Mass., 128
Plymouth Church of the Pilgrims, Brooklyn, N. Y., 115, 122, 123
Political abolitionists, 1840-1860, 30-31, 60, 83, 101-9
Polk, James K.: in election of 1844, 102
Portland, Me., 124; and Lovejoy's death, 48; abolitionist activity in, 72-73
Post Office Department: restriction on mails, attacked by abolitionists, 100-1
Power of Congress over the District of Columbia, The, 58
Presbyterian Church: emphasis on good works, 9; licenses Lovejoy to preach, 33; moderates fear reaction to Lovejoy's abolitionism, 35. *See also* Calvinism
Press, freedom of: defended by Lovejoy, 36, 38-39; claimed by abolitionists, 99-109 *passim*